CONTENTS

EINSTEIN

A BEGINNER'S GUIDE

JIM BREITHAUPT

Hodder & Stoughton

Acknowledgements

I would like to thank my family for their support in the preparation of this book, particularly my wife, Marie, for secretarial support and continued encouragement. I am also grateful to the publishing team at Hodder and Stoughton in particular Helen Green and Louise Crathorne who initiated and oversaw the project.

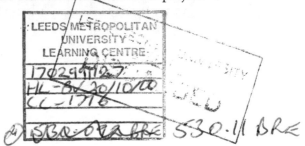
Orders: please contact Bookpoint Ltd, 39 Milton Park, Abingdon, Oxon OX14 4TD. Telephone: (44) 01235 827720, Fax: (44) 01235 400454. Lines are open from 9.00–6.00, Monday to Saturday, with a 24-hour message answering service. Email address: orders@bookpoint.co.uk

British Library Cataloguing in Publication Data
A catalogue record for this title is available from The British Library

ISBN 0 340 780436

First published 2000
Impression number   10 9 8 7 6 5 4 3 2
Year   2005 2004 2003 2002 2001 2000

Cartoons by Richard Chapman
Typeset by Transet Limited, Coventry, England.
Printed in Great Britain for Hodder & Stoughton Educational, a division of Hodder Headline Plc, 338 Euston Road, London NW1 3BH by Cox & Wyman, Reading, Berks

Contents

PREFACE

The life and work of Albert Einstein continues to fascinate people across the world, even though he died in 1955. This book aims to provide a gentle introduction to Einstein's theories on space, time, matter and energy, concentrating on the ideas that Einstein developed as well as considering the context in which he developed his ideas. The book is organized in 11 chapters, each dealing with a major aspect of Einstein's theories and linked together through the historical development of his ideas. Key facts and ideas are highlighted at intervals in each chapter, and each chapter concludes with a summary.

To separate Einstein's life story from his theories would not serve to convey in full the magnitude of Einstein's achievements and attributes. The story of the first 25 years of his life is perhaps extraordinary because there were few clues then about the revolutionary nature of the work he would go on to produce between 1905 and 1916. None of his relatives or friends would have predicted that the youthful Einstein would become the greatest scientist of the twentieth century, and perhaps the greatest for several more centuries to come. Einstein's theories of relativity discarded concepts that had been assumed, almost unquestioned, for thousands of years. Einstein provided a new understanding of space and time, and since then scientists and mathematicians have taken his work and developed it, finding new evidence to support his theories and making new predictions from them. Einstein caught the imagination of countless people in many countries, perhaps because of the mysterious nature of his theories, shrouded as they are in mathematical equations. They have led to enormously important results in science, and beyond science. Perhaps the most dramatic consequence of the ideas Einstein introduced has been to do with international politics and nuclear weapons, even though Einstein originally thought energy from nuclear reactions could not lead to such weapons. At the present time, the consequences of his work on special relativity continue to unfold as scientists strive to discover the fundamental nature of matter and energy, and his work on general relativity has provided the framework for the Big Bang Theory on the origin of the Universe. Read on to find out more about the awkward student who revolutionized the world of science.

Einstein in Perspective

Although many years have passed since Einstein published his theories of relativity, the consequences of his famous equation $E = mc^2$ have been profound. Using Einstein's ideas, scientists continue to make discoveries in cosmology about the Universe and in high-energy physics about matter deep inside every atom. Theoreticians continue to explore Einstein's ideas, making successful predictions of strange objects, such as black holes, and untested ideas such as wormholes in space-time. Many more years are likely to pass before the impact of Einstein's ideas can be assessed in full, just as happened after Sir Isaac Newton (1642–1727) whose work in the late seventeenth century revolutionized science and provided the foundations of science and engineering for the next two centuries.

Einstein hit the headlines in dramatic fashion in 1919, and rapidly achieved public recognition. Before 1919, although Einstein had shaken the foundations of physics with his theories of light, matter and energy, he was not widely known beyond the scientific communities in Europe and America. His peaceful lifestyle as a Professor of Physics in Berlin came to an abrupt end in November 1919 when the results of an astronomical investigation into predictions from his General Theory of Relativity were announced. The man who discovered that space could bend was invited to lecture in many countries and was hosted by world leaders and royalty. He became the most famous scientist of the twentieth century, his name a byword for brain power. In this chapter, we shall look at the events of 1919 that turned Einstein from a highly regarded scientist into a household name and earning him the enduring reputation of being one of the most brilliant scientists the world has ever known.

A CHALLENGING ASSUMPTION

Imagine a laser light show where beams of coloured light criss-cross the night sky. The show would be even more spectacular if the light beams could be bent and twisted into arcs and spirals as they passed through the air. In 1916, long before the invention of the laser, Einstein worked out that a light beam is bent by gravity but that the bending is usually too small to notice. The idea of gravity had been the brainchild of Sir Isaac Newton who had put forward the theory in the seventeenth century that a force of attraction exists between any two objects due to the mass of each object. To explain how this force acts between the two objects even though they are not in direct contact, Newton invented the idea of gravity acting at a distance between two objects. For example, a space probe on a flight path that passes a planet would crash on the planet if its path took it too close, pulled down by the planet's gravity. Newton took it for granted that space is an **absolute** quantity, the same everywhere and at all times. Perhaps Newton did ponder on the nature of the force of gravity between two objects, and maybe he thought about why two objects should affect each other, but his theory of gravity is essentially a statement that a force of gravity exists between any two objects, and that the force is stronger the closer the two objects are and the greater their respective masses.

Einstein challenged Newton's assumption that space is an absolute quantity that exists regardless of the presence or distribution of matter in the Universe. Nor did Einstein think much of Newton's assumption that time is also an absolute quantity, running at the same rate throughout the Universe. Einstein realized that space and time are characterized by **coordinates** used to locate events, and he sought to express the mathematical laws of physics in terms of general equations that apply to any system of coordinates. He brought gravity into his theory by linking it to accelerated motion and proceeded to demonstrate that space moves matter and matter curves space. We will look in more detail at these ideas in Chapters 6 and 7 of this book.

No other scientist before Einstein had even attempted the task Einstein set for himself: to develop a general theory of space, time and gravity. It was to take Einstein almost ten years of intense intellectual effort before he succeeded. He published his work in 1916 as the *The Foundation of the General Theory of Relativity* and used it to show that gravity can distort space, and alter the path of light. The Earth's gravity is too weak to distort space but Einstein predicted that light skimming the Sun is bent by a measurable amount by the Sun's gravity. This was a prediction that could be tested in a total solar eclipse. Few scientists at the time took much notice of Einstein's theory, probably because few had a sufficiently deep mathematical background to follow the complicated formulas and methods that Einstein had found necessary to use. Fortunately, Einstein's work reached Sir Arthur Eddington (1882–1944), Plumian Professor of Astronomy at the University of Cambridge and a mathematical genius.

THE ECLIPSE THAT ECLIPSED NEWTON

A total eclipse of the Sun generates enormous interest in those parts of the world on the path of totality. Such an eclipse happens when the Moon passes exactly in front of the Sun, causing the Sun to be blocked from view in the area where the Moon's shadow touches the Earth. Observers in the path of totality experience several minutes of darkness, providing invaluable moments for astronomers to observe and record the flaming gases of the solar corona that surrounds the Sun and cannot be seen during normal conditions. Total solar eclipses occur every few years, but totality covers a relatively small area of the surface of the Earth. The total eclipse of 1919 was the first total solar eclipse that scientists could use to test Einstein's prediction that gravity bends light.

Einstein had published his General Theory of Relativity in 1916 and had used it to predict that the Sun's gravity is capable of bending the path of light that skims the Sun from a distant star. The theory discards absolute space and time and leads to the conclusion that the shortest distance between two points in a region of space where gravity exists is not a straight line, and therefore that light follows a curve, not a straight line, when it passes through such a region. Few scientists at the time understood Einstein's theory but his prediction that gravity bends light could be tested by taking a photograph of the stars near the Sun during a total solar eclipse and comparing it with a photograph taken of the same stars in the night sky. The distorting effect of the Sun's gravity on the eclipse photograph would be apparent if the nearby stars appeared closer to the Sun than in the other photograph.

At the time Einstein published the General Theory of Relativity, Europe was in the midst of the Great War of 1914–1918. The armies of the British Empire, France, Russia and the other allied powers were locked in bitter conflict with the armies of Germany, Austria and the other central powers. Einstein's theory eventually reached Britain and, in March 1917, Sir Frank Dyson, the Astronomer Royal, persuaded the British government to fund expeditions to South America and West Africa to photograph the total solar eclipse due on 25 May 1919. The expedition to West Africa was led by Sir Arthur Eddington who was also Director of the Observatory at the University of Cambridge. Eddington and his group recorded the eclipse on 16 photographic film plates. Over the next few nights, Eddington developed the plates and found the distortion predicted by Einstein clearly evident on one plate. The photographic plates taken by the South American expedition were returned to Britain for development to obtain better pictures than could be obtained on location. The decision to return the photographic plates to Britain for development proved wise as seven plates were found to show the predicted displacement of stars near the Sun. The good news reached Einstein in late September 1919 as a telegram, 'Eddington found star displacement at Sun', sent from Holland by fellow physicist, Hendrik Lorentz (1853–1928). The news filtered out slowly to the wider scientific community. The Royal Society and the Royal

Astronomical Society in London met on 6 November 1919 to hear Dyson's reports of the expedition and their results. J.J. Thomson, President of the Royal Society, stated that Einstein's General Theory of Relativity ranks as 'one of the greatest achievements in the history of human thought – a whole new continent of ideas'. The next day, *The Times* reported the conference and stated in an article, entitled 'The Fabric of the Universe', that the scientific conception of the Universe must be changed. In Berlin Einstein acquired instant fame worldwide. He was swamped by reporters, received sacks of letters and innumerable requests for newspaper articles and lecture tours. He responded to invitations to visit Britain and America and other countries, meeting countless politicians, Church leaders as well as other scientists. His informal manner and popular expositions of his work endeared him to people in all walks of life even though few could understand his theory. Perhaps the newness of his ideas appealed to people after the grim war years as they flocked to lecture halls to hear scientists explain why his theory changed our perception of the Universe.

Einstein discovered that fame is a double-edged sword, bringing problems as well as honours and influence. Einstein disliked nationalism and was a pacifist during the Great War. His General Theory of Relativity was attacked by a group of German scientists, led by Philipp Lenard who had been awarded the Nobel prize in 1905 for his investigations on electron beams or 'cathode rays' as they were then called. The 'anti-relativity company', as Einstein called them, attracted the support of right-wing nationalists who were attempting to undermine the German government. Einstein became a target of anti-Semitism in defeated Germany. In 1920, he and his supporters in the scientific world confronted the anti-relativity scientists at a conference in Germany guarded by armed police. The outcome failed to convince the anti-relativists but the support from his friends persuaded Einstein to remain in Germany instead of moving to a safer position abroad. Nevertheless, the hostility he experienced made him more aware than most that the political climate in Germany was turning hostile. On a visit to Prague in 1921 he confided to a fellow scientist that he might be forced to emigrate from Germany within ten years. In 1933, he left Germany for America and never returned.

Einstein was awarded the 1921 Nobel prize for physics as a result of his 1905 paper on the interaction between **radiation** and matter. The theory he put forward here had been tested successfully by experiments and also had practical applications. The General Theory of

KEYWORD

Radiation: energy that is carried by waves as they travel through a substance or space.

Relativity was not regarded at that stage as sufficiently proven by the awards committee. However, over the next two decades, Einstein's stature and influence grew. By the end of the twentieth century, Einstein's predictions from the General Theory of Relativity had been confirmed precisely in a large number of experiments and observations. There is little doubt that Einstein's General Theory of Relativity is a giant leap in mankind's progress towards a better understanding of the Universe and our place in it. We shall look in more detail at this theory and the evidence for it in the later chapters of this book after considering how Einstein progressed towards the theory, taking in his extremely important work on Special Relativity which in itself represented a big step forward.

✳ ✳ ✳ ✳SUMMARY ✳ ✳ ✳ ✳

• The General Theory of Relativity, published by Einstein in 1916, expresses the laws of physics in terms of equations that apply to any system of coordinates. The theory predicted that light grazing the Sun from nearby stars is deflected by the Sun's gravity.

• The 1919 solar eclipse was used to successfully test Einstein's General Theory of Relativity by measuring on photographic plates the displacement of stars near the Sun during the eclipse.

Unusual Ideas

Einstein's progress from schoolboy to student to scientist reveals few clues about the turmoil that his scientific theories would bring to the complacent world of physics at the start of the twentieth century. He failed to distinguish himself as a student, perhaps because his ideas were so different from what was required to pass his exams. Maybe his scientific theories of 1905 would not have emerged had he stayed on at university after he graduated in 1900.

FROM REBEL TO REVOLUTIONARY

For the first 25 years of his life, no one would have guessed that Einstein was to become the greatest scientist of the twentieth century. As a result of the failure of his father's electrical business, his family moved from Ulm to Munich in southwest Germany in 1880, less than a year after his birth. Einstein attended a Catholic school in Munich from age five to age ten when he gained a place at the Luipold Gymnasium, a Munich secondary school in Munich where he remained until he was 16. His parents were from a non-orthodox Jewish background, and held few traces of the Prussian authoritarianism that dominated the new German Empire at that time. At secondary school, he was bored by most subjects and disliked the regimented system of education that prevailed in Germany at that time. Not unlike most teenagers, he resented and questioned authority, although at home he was a good child and presented few problems for his parents. Max Talmey, a medical student and family friend encouraged his interest in maths and physics. His school career in Munich ended prematurely when his father's business failed yet again and his family moved to Milan in 1894. Einstein was supposed to remain in Munich to complete his school course in the care of a relative but he was regarded as a disruptive presence and fell foul of the school authorities. He and his teachers parted company with no regrets. His father wanted him to train as an electrical engineer, but without a school diploma he could not apply to any universities in Germany. One way forward was for him to sit the annual entrance examination of the Swiss Federal Institute of Technology (known as the ETH), in Zurich. He sent an essay of his thoughts about electromagnetic fields and light waves to his wealthy uncle, Caesar Koch, perhaps aware that he would need financial support if he was to study in Zurich. His family recognized his unusual mathematical talents and arranged for him to sit the ETH entrance examination but he failed the papers in languages and biology. However, the principal was impressed with Einstein's maths paper, particularly as Einstein was two years younger than most of the candidates. Einstein was sent to a nearby high school to prepare for the following year's examination at ETH. He responded well to the general atmosphere in the school, where the discipline was much lighter than in his previous school and he gained a place at the ETH on the four-year physics course starting in October 1896 after persuading his family to allow him to switch into physics from electrical engineering.

During his year preparing for the ETH examination, Einstein decided he no longer wished to remain a German national, perhaps as a result of his secondary education at a strict and formal school in Munich. With some reluctance, his father wrote to the appropriate authorities in Ulm and Einstein became a stateless person. At the ETH, he was a typical student. It was here that he made life-long friends and also met his wife-to-be, Mileva Marich. In his spare time, he developed a passion for sailing and he studied the works of scientists and mathematicians that were not part of his course, perhaps left out because his professors considered the works to be too advanced for students to consider.

He was particularly interested in the work of Ernst Mach (1838–1916), an Austrian physicist and philosopher, who regarded absolute space as a meaningless concept. Einstein developed a reputation among the professors as an awkward student, always asking difficult questions. He graduated in 1900, stateless and without a job to go to, having been rejected by ETH for a post at the lowest level of academic life in the institution, unlike some of his fellow students who were kept on. He worked on and off in Switzerland as a temporary teacher for two years, gaining Swiss citizenship in 1901. At last, in June 1902, he obtained a job in Berne as a Patent Officer. He settled into a daily routine of undemanding work, advising and reporting on patent applications and the associated legal requirements. In his job, he learned how to analyse machines and to write carefully and precisely about them, thus gaining skills that were to prove valuable in his later career. In addition, he had access to the Patent Office Library and he used his spare time to pursue research interests in physics. Between 1901 and 1905, Einstein produced some minor papers on molecular theory in which he sought out the underlying links between different experiments. His marriage to Mileva in 1903 was followed in due course by the birth of his first son, Hans Albert.

Physics at that time was emerging as a subject with fundamental difficulties inherent to it that were beyond the range of the well-established classical laws and theories. The discovery of the **electron** by British physicist J.J. Thomson (1856–1940) in Cambridge upset the theory that atoms are indivisible, for the electron seemed to be part of the atom but no one had worked out what the rest of the atom contained. Eminent scientists of the time held the view that atoms were no more than theoretical entities and there was no direct evidence for their existence. Radioactivity had just been discovered by

KEYWORDS

Electron: a negatively charged particle contained in every atom. All atoms contain a positively charged nucleus which is where most of the mass of the atom is concentrated.

Thermal radiation: electromagnetic waves emitted by a hot object; consists of infrared radiation and light.

Antoine Becquerel (1852–1988) in France and scientists such as Marie Curie (1867–1934) in Paris and Ernest Rutherford (1837–1931), then in Manchester, were puzzled about the nature and cause of the radiation from so-called radioactive substances such as uranium and radium.

Another problem that led to a rethink of the classical theories of physics related to **thermal radiation** from an object at constant temperature. In 1899 Otto Lummer and Ernst Pringsheim in Germany had made precise

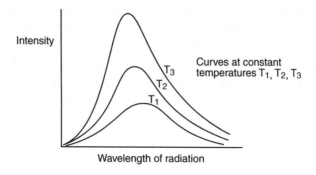

Figure 1: Thermal radiation curves

measurements of the distribution of the radiation intensity at different wavelengths and found the intensity peaked at a certain wavelength, as shown in Figure 1. The continuous range of wavelengths was expected as it was known that thermal radiation is **electromagnetic radiation** which covers a continuous range of wavelengths including radio waves, infrared radiation, light, ultraviolet radiation and X-rays. However, the existence of an intensity peak was not in accordance with the laws of classical physics which predicted that the

KEYWORD

Electromagnetic radiation: electromagnetic waves, including radio waves, microwaves, infrared radiation, light, ultraviolet, X-rays and gamma rays. All electromagnetic waves travel through space at speed of 300,000 km/s. This speed is denoted by the symbol c.

intensity became higher and higher at shorter and shorter wavelengths. This prediction was at odds with the results obtained by Lummer and Pringsheim, and the problem became known as the 'ultraviolet catastrophe' because the classical theory predicted that the intensity tends to infinity in the ultraviolet region of the electromagnetic spectrum. The solution was worked out by German physicist Max Planck (1858–1947) in Berlin who introduced the completely new concept of quantization of energy to arrive at his solution. Planck's solution was based on the assumption that the energy of a vibrating atom in a solid can only be equal to a multiple of a basic amount. He introduced the word 'quantum' for this basic amount and showed that the shape of the radiation curve can be explained if the quantum of energy is assumed to be proportional to the frequency of the vibrating atom. The quantum theory invented by Planck meant that energy at an atomic level is lumpy and is not distributed evenly, as the classical laws stated it should be. Planck was to feature prominently in Einstein's career after 1905, one of the first major scientists to recognize Einstein's potential.

Unsolved problems in physics near the end of the 19th century

✳ Atoms: what are they made of?

✳ Radioactivity: what is it and what causes it?

✳ Radiation: why does the classical theory not explain the spectrum of radiation from a hot object?

EINSTEIN, THE PROBLEM SOLVER

Between 1901–1905, Einstein developed his ideas on energy and matter, motion and space; and space and time. Working in isolation from mainstream researchers, he published three important papers in 1905 on theoretical physics, two of which alone would have earned Einstein's place in the history of physics as an important scientist for resolving outstanding issues in physics. The third paper however was to throw the certainties of classical physics into complete turmoil.

Brownian motion

The existence of **molecules** was proved by Einstein's explanation of the erratic motion of particles such as pollen grains in water or smoke particles in air. This type of motion was discovered almost a century earlier by Scottish

KEYWORD

Molecule: atom, or two or more atoms joined together.

botanist Robert Brown (1773–1858), who used a microscope to observe the particles. He found that the particles seemed to quiver continuously and move about unpredictably, as if they were alive. He tested **inorganic particles** and found the type of motion which became known as Brownian motion. Einstein was fascinated by the effect when he first observed it and he wanted to find what was causing it. He explained it by assuming that the particles were continually being struck by fast-moving molecules of the surrounding liquid or gas, too small to see directly but nevertheless capable of noticeably shifting the particles. He worked out that the tiny particles were being struck unevenly and at random by much smaller molecules with a wide range of speeds, buffeting the particles about at random. He showed

KEYWORDS

Inorganic particles: originally defined as a substance not from a living system; now defined as a substance with no molecules in it containing carbon atoms.

Photoelectricity: emission of electrons from a metal caused by eletromagnetic radiation.

Refraction: the change of direction of light on passing from one transparent medium to another.

that measurements on the motion of the particles could be used to calculate the mass of a single molecule and the number of molecules per unit volume. After this paper appeared, doubts about the existence of atoms and molecules were finally laid to rest.

Photons

The explanation of **photoelectricity** was another scientific puzzle settled by Einstein in the second of the 1905 papers. The nature of light had fascinated scientists ever since Newton had put forward the corpuscular theory of light in which he held that light is composed of tiny particles he called corpuscles. He used the theory to explain the law of reflection of a light ray on a mirror by supposing that the corpuscles bounced off the mirror without loss of speed, just as a squash ball does when it hits a smooth wall. Newton also explained the phenomenon of **refraction** of light which is the change of direction of a light ray when it passes from air into a transparent substance such as glass. According to Newton, the corpuscles gain speed on entering the transparent substance, pulled in by an attractive force at the surface. This causes any light ray directed non-perpendicularly at the surface to change direction towards the perpendicular on entering the substance. The opposite effect happens when a light ray emerges from a substance into air. This change of direction is the reason why a swimming pool or river often looks shallower than it really is. Newton's theory of light was challenged by Dutch physicist Christiaan Huygens (1625–1698) who put forward the wave theory of light. Huygens imagined that light from a point source spreads out in much the same way as water waves spread out on the surface of a pond when a stone is dropped onto the pond. His theory explained reflection and refraction although, to make the waves refract in the observed direction, it was necessary to assume light slows down on entering a transparent substance. Which theory was correct? No evidence existed at that time to prove that the speed of light in a transparent substance is more or less than in air, and so Newton's theory prevailed because he was the most eminent scientist of his era.

A century before Einstein began to pose questions about the speed of light, evidence for the wave theory of light was discovered by English physicist Thomas Young (1773–1829) at the Royal Institution in London. Young observed light from a narrow source through two close-

KEYWORD

Diffraction: the spreading of waves round an obstacle or through a gap.

ly spaced parallel slits in an opaque plate. He found a pattern of bright and dark bands of light (referred to as 'fringes') was formed with a spacing that depended on the distance between the two parallel slits. Newton's theory predicted just two fringes should be formed, one for each of the two slits but Young found there was always more than two. Huygens wave theory provided an explanation based on the idea that light waves from one slit reinforced light waves from the other slit at certain positions (the bright fringes) and cancelled out at other positions (the dark fringes). Scientists found this hard to accept because light waves would sweep round obstacles, making clear shadows impossible. Several decades passed before this effect, known as **diffraction**, was observed. Perhaps more significantly, the speed of light in water was measured and found to be less than in air. So Huygens had been correct after all. Wave theory was extended by Scottish physicist James Clerk Maxwell (1831–1879), who produced a theory of electromagnetic waves that proved that light is a small part of the spectrum of electromagnetic waves. Two decades after Maxwell died, the German physicist Gustav Hertz (1887–1975), discovered radio waves at the long wavelength end of the electromagnetic spectrum and another German physicist Wilhelm Röntgen (1845–1923) discovered X-rays at the other end. The theory of electromagnetic waves was a triumph of classical physics and led directly to a wide range of technological applications, including broadcasting and X-ray imaging. However, Planck's quantum theory called into question the classical theory as it meant that an atom absorbs or emits electromagnetic waves in packets, each packet being a quantum of energy. Planck thought the quanta emitted by an atom joined up to form a continuous wave so he was able to reconcile his quantum theory with the classical theory of electromagnetic waves.

However, in 1900, the classical theory received a setback as a result of a detailed investigation by Lenard of the phenomenon of photoelectricity which had been discovered a decade earlier. Photoelectricity is the emission of electrical charge from a metal plate when it is illuminated by visible or ultraviolet light. Lenard concluded that the charge is carried by electrons which leave the metal when they gain energy from the light directed at the metal. However, he found to his surprise that the effect did not happen if the light frequency was below a certain value that depended on the particular metal used. The reason for his surprise was that the classical theory of waves predicted the effect should happen at any frequency of light. None of Lenard's contemporaries could explain the existence of a threshold frequency below which the effect did not happen.

The challenge was taken up by Einstein in 1905 who invented the photon theory of light to explain the effect. Einstein, an obscure patent officer outside any university department at that time, put forward the concept of the photon as the quantum of electromagnetic radiation, emitted like 'a flying needle' when an atom released energy. The energy, E, of a single photon depends on the radiation frequency, f, in accordance with the equation: $E = hf$, where h is a constant that Planck introduced into his explanation of thermal radiation, and is known as the Planck constant.

In the photoelectric effect, a single electron at the metal surface absorbs a single **photon** and gains its energy, hf. Since the electron needs a certain amount of energy to leave the metal, it can only do so if the energy it gains from a photon is greater than the amount needed to leave the metal. If the radiation frequency is below the threshold frequency for the metal, no electron in the metal can gain sufficient energy from a photon to leave the metal. The

KEYWORD

Photon: a packet of electromagnetic waves. The energy of a photon depends on the frequence of the waves. An electron in an atom emits a photon when it moves to a lower energy level in the atom.

simplicity of Einstein's explanation of the photoelectric effect stunned the scientific community. They wanted more experimental evidence and held back from accepting the photon theory until 1913 when Robert Millikan in America carried out conclusive tests. Einstein's theory that light is 'lumpy' was confirmed and in 1921, the Nobel prize was awarded to Einstein for his explanation of the photoelectric effect. Einstein was not put off by the initial lack of encouragement and the third of his important 1905 papers on Special Relativity was published a short time later. This paper was more revolutionary than the others and it was to propel Einstein from obscurity to the forefront of the world's scientific community within a few years. We shall look in more detail at Einstein's revolutionary ideas on Special Relativity in the next chapter.

✳ ✳ ✳ ✳SUMMARY ✳ ✳ ✳ ✳

● New discoveries in physics at the end of the nineteenth century: X-Rays, electrons, radioactivity.

● Unsolved problems at the end of the nineteenth century: nature of radioactivity; structure of the atom; thermal radiation spectrum.

● Einstein's 1905 theories:

1 the explanation of Brownian motion;

2 the photon theory and the explanation of photoelectricity;

3 the theory of Special Relativity.

On the Move

As a student, Einstein thought about how the world would appear to an observer travelling at the speed of light. He knew that light is an electromagnetic wave, which at the time was thought to be carried by vibrations of the ether, an invisible substance that was supposed to fill space. Yet no experimental evidence could be found for the existence of the ether and without the ether, how could the motion of an object through space be detected? Einstein hit upon the solution to these problems in 1905 through a new approach that no one else had considered.

THE EXPERIMENT THAT DIDN'T WORK

How can you tell if something is moving? At this moment, you are rushing through space on planet Earth at a speed of about 30 kilometres per second (km/s). In the time it has taken you to read this sentence, you will have moved more than 100 km through space. If Earth was covered in cloud, would it be possible to tell if the Earth is moving? In 1888, Albert Michelson and Edward Morley in America carried out an experiment to try to detect the presence of the ether surrounding the Earth by comparing the speed of light in the direction of the Earth's motion with the speed of light perpendicular to the Earth's motion. According to the classical laws of motion discovered by Galileo (1564–1642) and developed by Newton in the seventeenth century:

* light should travel faster when it is moving in the same direction as the Earth compared to when it is moving perpendicular to the direction of motion of the Earth, not unlike swimming with the current in a river compared to swimming across the current;

* light should travel slower when it is moving in the opposite direction to the Earth compared to when it is moving perpendicular to the direction of motion of the Earth, not unlike swimming against the current in a river compared to swimming across the current.

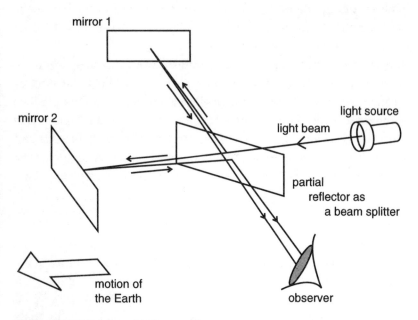

Figure 2: The Michelson–Morley experiment

Michelson and Morley devised an experiment to compare the time taken by light to travel a certain distance parallel to the Earth's motion to a mirror and back, with the time taken to travel the same distance perpendicular to the Earth's motion. Using the classical laws of motion, they calculated that light travelling to a mirror and back should take less time if its direction was parallel to the Earth's direction of motion than if its direction was perpendicular to the Earth's direction of motion. They worked out that the difference should be large enough to measure with their apparatus but when they did the experiment, no such difference could be detected. This null result meant that the motion of the Earth through space had no effect on the speed of light, as if a river swimmer is unaffected by the river flow.

The existence of the ether as the substance carrying light was thus thrown into doubt. To explain the null effect, Hendrik Lorentz in Holland and George Fitzgerald in Ireland put forward the idea that when light is travelling parallel to the Earth's motion the distance between the light source and the mirror was shortened due to the Earth's motion through the ether, just sufficiently enough to make produce the null result. They worked out that a rod of length L_s when stationary was shortened to a length L_s/γ when it moves at a speed υ in the direction of the Earth's motion, where $\gamma = 1/\sqrt{(1-\upsilon^2/c^2)}$ and c is the speed of light in space. As shown on page 86, the factor γ, known as the Lorentz factor, is always greater than 1 except when $\upsilon=0$ when it is equal to 1, thus making a rod shorter when it is moving than when it is at rest. It was introduced with no justification other than it gave the null result – a fiddle factor if ever there was one!

SPECIAL RELATIVITY

Einstein may not have thought much about the Michelson–Morley result, but he did know that the classical laws of mechanics and of electro-magnetic waves were not the same for any two observers moving at different speeds. He was particularly concerned that the equations used to describe the progress of electromagnetic waves differed for a stationary observer and a moving observer, implying that electromagnetic

KEYWORDS

Frame of reference: a rigid body used to define a system of coordinates.

Inertial frame of reference: a frame of reference in which an object at rest in that frame remains at rest, provided no forces act on it.

waves could be used to tell if an observer is moving. Also, if the speed of light was dependent on the speed of the observer, it would be possible in theory to catch up with light. Einstein thought about how the world would appear to someone riding on a light beam, moving at the speed of light. Simultaneous events would no longer appear simultaneous. For example, in a duel where an observer sees two people shoot at each other at the same time, would another observer travelling almost at the speed of light see one gun fired before the other? Einstein realized that distances and time intervals are determined by events and are not absolute quantities. The location and time of an event may be specified with respect to a local reference position and a local reference time. Einstein wanted to know how the distance and time between two separate events would differ for two observers moving at different velocities. Each observer can be thought of as being in a **frame of reference** in which a free object at rest remains at rest. This is called an **inertial frame of reference**.

Einstein decided that two key assumptions always held in any inertial frame of reference.

✳ The speed of light in free space, c, is **invariant**, which means that c has the same value, regardless of the motion of the source or of the observer.

✳ The laws of physics expressed as equations should always take the same form.

The first assumption means that a pulse of light emitted by a light source always travels away from the light source at a speed of 300,000 km/s, regardless of how fast the source is moving or its direction. For example, if a light source on a space ship moving at a speed of 200,000 km/s emits a light pulse in the same direction as the direction of motion of the space ship, the light pulse would move a distance of 300,000 km/s not 500,000 km/s. An observer on the space ship would also see the light pulse move ahead a distance of 300,000 km/s. This seems to defy common sense. On a train moving forward at a speed of 2 m/s, someone walking at a speed of 3 m/s to the front of the train would travel 3 m along the train every second. However, an observer beside the track would see the walker move 5 m along the train every second because the train moves forward 2 m every second.

KEYWORDS

Invariant: means 'does not change' i.e. stays the same.

Transformation rules: method of changing the coordinates of a point written in terms of one system of coordinates to another system, in the same way that a map reference given in miles could be converted to one given in kilometres.

The second assumption means any equation written in terms of a system of coordinates of an inertial frame of reference should be capable of being transformed into an identical equation in terms of the coordinates of any other inertial frame of reference. Einstein showed that the **transformation rules** worked out by Galileo and by Newton do not allow equations that describe the progress of electromagnetic waves to be transformed. Einstein worked out the correct transformation equations and he showed how the Lorentz factor from page 19 arises. See also Appendix 1 for further explanation of this. Thus Einstein showed that all inertial frames of reference are equivalent and that there is no preferred frame. In other words, absolute space and time are meaningless as nature does not provide us with a preferred frame of reference. All motion is relative and absolute motion cannot be detected.

Einstein presented his work in the third of his 1905 papers, entitled ' On the Electrodynamics of Moving Objects'. This, and a further short paper about mass and energy published later in the year, became known as the 'Theory of Special Relativity'. The significance of Einstein's work was not recognized by many scientists in 1905 and there was no experimental evidence to support it. However, Planck in Berlin drew attention to Einstein's ideas in his own lectures and in 1907, Einstein was invited to take up a part-time position at the University of Berne, still working full-time at the Patent Office. Within two years, Einstein had made his first appearance at a major scientific conference and had been appointed to a full-time professorship at the University of Zurich, partly as a result of wider publicity gained for Einstein's work by his former ETH mathematics teacher, Hermann Minowski, who introduced the concept of space time into relativity theory.

STRETCHING AND SHRINKING
Let's consider two of the consequences of Einstein's Theory of Special Relativity at this stage:

1 A moving clock runs slower than a stationary clock
If two identical clocks are synchronized at the same place (i.e. both set to zero and started at the same place and time) and one clock is taken off on a high-speed journey at constant speed v, then returned at the same speed, it reads less than the stationary clock on return. This effect is known as time dilation. Einstein showed that the two readings, t_M for the moving clock and t_s for the stationary clock, are related by the equation:

$t_s = \gamma \, t_M$, where γ is the Lorentz factor (see page 86), equal to $1/\sqrt{(1-v^2/c^2)}$ and c is the speed of light.

For example, for $v = 0.6$ c, then $\gamma = 1.25$ and so $t_s = 1.25t_M$; if the moving clock showed 04.00 hours on return, the stationary clock would show 05.00 hours. If this seems odd, remember time is not an absolute quantity and the time interval between two events depends on the motion of the observer observing the events – remember the duellists on page 19.

A tale of two twins

According to the above equation, if a twin, aged 21, takes off on a high-speed round trip in a space rocket at Lorentz factor 1.25 s/he will return four years later aged 25. The other twin who stays on Earth will be 26 when the traveller twin returns. This might seem odd, but there is plenty of scientific evidence to support the theory. The most direct evidence has come from the **atomic clock**, which is remarkably accurate and reliable. An atomic clock flown round the world in a jet plane has a Lorentz factor almost but not quite equal to 1, just great enough to make a significant difference between it and a stationary clock. Precise measurements on atomic clocks support the theory that a moving clock falls behind a stationary one. Hence the travelling twin returns home younger than the 'stay-at-home twin'.

Moving objects appear to contract

A rod moving at constant speed in a fixed direction appears to be shorter than if it was stationary. Einstein showed that the observed length $L = L_s/\gamma$, where L_s is the length of the rod when stationary (i.e. its proper length). For example, a rocket ship 1000 m in length moving at a speed of 0.6 c would appear to be only 800 m (where c is the speed of light) because its Lorentz factor of 1.25 would make its observed length equal to $(1000/1.25)$ m.

KEYWORD

Atomic clock: contains a crystal consisting of atoms of a certain type that vibrate at a constant frequency. The scientific unit of time, the second is defined in terms of a certain number of vibrations of the atoms of a particular type of crystal.

Why should this be so? The time taken for the rocket ship to pass an observer is equal to L /ʋ, its observed length divided by its speed ʋ. The rocket crew would measure a time for this interval equal to $(L_s/ʋ)$.

Since the crew's clock is stationary relative to the rocket, whereas the observer's clock is moving relative to the rocket, then applying $t_s = \gamma\, t_M$ gives $L_s/ʋ = \gamma\, L/ʋ$. Multiplying both sides of this equation by ʋ gives $L_s = \gamma\, L$, which gives $L = L_s/\gamma$ when rearranged.

The high-speed tube train

Could a high-speed train be trapped in a shorter tunnel if its length is contracted due to its speed? Suppose a train 110 m in length moves so fast that its length appears to be just 100 m. A Lorentz factor of 1.1 would be needed for this, corresponding to a speed of 0.42 c. Could the train be trapped in a 100 m tunnel? A door operator at the tunnel entrance could be ready to close the tunnel the instant the back end of the train enters the tunnel. The front end would appear to be at the tunnel exit at this instant. However, a light signal from this door operator would take time to reach the door operator at the exit end. The front end of the train would be out by then.

The scientific community was slow to recognize Einstein's special theory of relativity, perhaps because there was little experimental evidence to support it and the ideas were revolutionary. At his first real meeting with other physicists at a conference in 1909, Einstein delivered a paper on the nature of light in which he used his relativity theory to support and develop his photon theory of light. Shortly after the conference, Einstein was appointed to the post of Associate Professor at the University of Zurich. After almost a decade as an outsider, Einstein became a full-time academic and was able to leave the Patent Office. During the next decade, he was to produce an even more astounding theory which was to confirm his authority as the most famous scientist of our age. However, even without this later work, his discoveries about mass and energy were to have immense military and political consequences.

✳ ✳ ✳ ✳ SUMMARY ✳ ✳ ✳ ✳

• The Michelson–Morley Experiment could not detect the effect of the Earth's motion on the speed of light.

• The Theory of Special Relativity assumes:

  – the speed of light in free space is always the same, regardless of the motion of the observer or the light source;

  – the laws of physics expressed as equations should always take the sane form in any inertial frame of reference.

• Consequences of Special Relativity:

  – time dilation – a moving clock runs slower than a stationary clock;

  – length contraction – a moving rod appears shorter than if it was at rest.

The Most Famous Equation in Physics: E=mc²

Before Einstein, the nature of space and time had been questioned by several eminent scientists and mathematicians, including Henri Poincaré (1854–1912) in France as well as Fitzgerald and Lorentz (see page 18). Einstein's revolutionary relativity paper of 1905 (see page 19) showed that the length of an object is not a fundamental property of the object as it depends on the velocity of the observer of the object. The paper also led to the conclusion that the time interval between two events is not an absolute quantity as it also depends on the velocity of the observer of the events. Until Einstein showed the way forward, the leading researchers had been stumbling to understand experimental findings such as the null result from the Michelson–Morley experiment (see page 17). As if this was not enough, a further aspect of Einstein's ideas on relativity was to reveal a link between mass and energy, a link that no other scientist or mathematician even suspected. The consequences of this discovery by Einstein were to resound through the twentieth century, and will continue to do so for centuries to come.

MASS AND ENERGY

Before 1905, matter was matter and energy was energy. Two key principles established in the nineteenth century still underpinned physics and chemistry at the start of the twentieth century.

The Principle of Conservation of Mass

This means that in any situation where a change takes place, the total mass of all the substances present after the change is equal to the total mass before the change. This principle was supported by countless experiments, and chemists still use it extensively to calculate how much mass of a compound or element is produced when known amounts of other compounds or elements react.

The Principle of Conservation of Energy

This principle had been established in the middle of the nineteenth century as a result of investigations carried out by scientists, such as James Prescott Joule (1818–1889) in England who demonstrated that the total energy of an isolated system remains constant when energy is transferred from one part of the system to other parts. The unit of energy, the joule, was named after Joule, as a tribute to his work. One joule is the energy released by a one watt light bulb in one second.

To appreciate the link between energy and mass developed and formulated by Einstein, let's consider the scientific meaning of each of these words.

Mass

This is a measure of how much matter is present in an object. An important property of an object due to its mass is its **inertia**, which is its resistance to change of motion. A moving object is more difficult to stop the larger its mass is. The masses of two objects may be compared by applying the same force to each object one at a time and observing which object attains a certain speed fastest. As we shall see later in this chapter, Einstein moved away from the concept of mass as a fixed quantity and showed that the mass of an object depends on its speed.

Energy

This is the capacity of a body to force an object to move. A moving body possesses **energy** because if it crashes into another object that is free to move, it makes the object move. The energy of a moving body is called kinetic energy. In the above example, the moving body slows down or stops and so it loses kinetic energy; the other object gains kinetic energy because it moves. In the collision, heat and sound may be created. The energy converted to heat and sound is equal to the difference between the kinetic energy before the collision and the kinetic energy after the collision.

KEYWORDS

Inertia: property of an object due to its mass; a measure of the difficulty of changing its speed or direction.

Energy: the capacity of an object to work on another object by forcing it to move.

The kinetic energy of a moving body depends on the mass and the speed of the body. To make a body reach a certain speed from a resting point in a certain time, the body needs to be acted on by a certain force. Imagine a space rocket launched by accelerating it up a long, straight, uphill track so it flies off the end of the track into space. The speed the rocket reaches at the top of the track would depend on the force, the duration of time for which the force acts, and the mass of the rocket. The ground crew would measure a longer duration of time than the rocket crew would measure because of time dilation (see page 21), yet the speed reached would be the same. How can this be so? The answer is because the mass of a moving object increases as it speeds up. The longer time measured by the rocket crew is because the rocket mass increased during the launch.

After the publication of his 1905 paper on Brownian motion (see page 11), Einstein showed in a short follow-up paper that the mass, m, of a moving object depends on its speed v, in accordance with the equation $m = \gamma m_0$, where γ is the Lorentz factor equal to $1/\sqrt{(1 - v^2/c^2)}$ and c is the speed of light. The quantity m_0 is the rest mass of the object which is its mass as measured by an observer who is at rest relative to the object. He then used his mass formula to show that the energy of an object, E, and its mass are related by the equation $E = mc^2$.

> $E = mc^2$ could have been figured out several years before Einstein if evidence recently found in Italy is validated. Even so, Einstein proved it rigorously and explained its meaning thoroughly.

THE COSMIC SPEED LIMIT

The increase of mass with speed is shown in Figure 3 (see page 28). The graph has been plotted using Einstein's formula $m = m_0/\sqrt{(1-v^2/c^2)}$ for different values v in terms of c. Using this formula, you can show that an object needs to be travelling at a speed of:

* over 40% of the speed of light to increase its mass to 10% more than its rest mass;

* 80% of the speed of light to increase its mass 67% more than its rest mass;

* 99% of the speed of light to increase its mass to over 7 times its rest mass;

* 99.99% of the speed of light to increase its mass to over 70 times its rest mass.

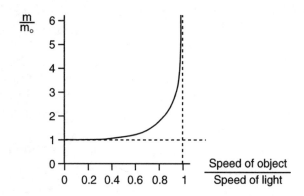

Figure 3: Mass v speed

No object can be accelerated to reach the speed of light as its mass would become infinite at the speed of light and this is physically impossible. Why should the mass of an object depend on its speed? Mass is a measure of the inertia of an object, its resistance to change of its motion. The faster an object moves, the greater its resistance to change of its motion. Einstein showed from his mass formula $m = m_0/\sqrt{(1-v^2/c^2)}$ that the kinetic energy gained by an object when it is accelerated from rest to a certain speed v is equal to $mc^2-m_0c^2$. He realized that m_0c^2 is energy due to the rest mass of the object, thus concluding that:

* the rest mass of an object represents energy locked up by an object due to its rest mass;

* the total energy (E) of an object is equal to mc^2 which is the sum of its rest mass energy plus energy supplied to it.

Thus Einstein arrived at his famous equation $E = mc^2$, unaware of its full significance which was not to be realized for several more decades. To appreciate the significance of this equation, consider the following: the energy released by burning 1 kg of fuel is no more than about 50 million joules, about the same as the energy released by a 100 watt light bulb illuminated for six days continuously. Given that the speed of light, c is 300 million metres per second, prove for yourself that the total energy of a 1 kg mass is equal to 90,000 million million joules ($= mc^2 = 1 \times 300$ million $\times 300$ million joules), enough to keep almost 30 million 100 watt light bulbs illuminated for a year. However, this energy release can only happen if all the mass is annihilated and changed into energy, a process which Einstein in 1905 reckoned to be impossible.

> If an object is supplied with energy, its mass increases on a scale given by $E = mc^2$. The mass of an object tends to infinity as its speed approaches the speed of light. No object (other than a photon) can travel as fast as light because it cannot have an infinite amount of energy.

ENERGY FROM THE NUCLEUS

For many years, Einstein did not think that energy could be released on the enormous scale indicated by $E = mc^2$, approximately 90,000 million million joules for every kilogramme of matter that could be annihilated. Rutherford, who discovered the nucleus of the atom and is therefore the originator of nuclear physics, didn't think so either, and is reported to have described the prospects of nuclear energy on a large scale as 'moonshine'. Einstein and Rutherford and their contemporaries realized that when energy is released from any isolated system, the total mass of the system afterwards is less than the total mass before the energy was released. They knew that the mass difference Δm is equal is to E/c^2, here E is the energy released. This difference is far too small to measure in chemical changes or when energy is stored mechanically, for example in a stretched spring. A sealed torch that operates at a power of 10 watts releases 10 joules of light energy every second. Suppose such a torch could operate continuously for a year so it would release over 300 million joules of light energy in that time. What would be its mass changes as a result? Using $E = mc^2$, its mass change would be about 0.003 millionths of a kilogramme (= 300 million joules/300 million metres per second^2) which is about three millionths of a gramme – far too small to measure!

However, Einstein, Rutherford and other scientists did know that the energy released when the nuclei of light elements fuse together causes measurable mass loss. For example, it was known that a helium nucleus consists of two neutrons and two protons and it was discovered that the mass of a helium nucleus is about 0.8% less than the mass of two protons and two neutrons. This mass difference is because the protons and neutrons in a nucleus are locked together, unable to be freed unless supplied with sufficient energy to overcome the strong nuclear force that binds them together. To pull a helium nucleus apart, energy would need to be supplied to pull the neutrons and protons away from each other. This energy would be converted to mass, so increasing the mass of the protons and neutrons by 0.8%. For many years, it was thought that nuclear energy could only be released by radioactive decay which is the natural disintegration of unstable nuclei. Marie Curie and other scientists had investigated the properties of naturally occuring radioactive elements such as uranium and had discovered new elements which were radioactive. All these radioactive substances release energy due to nuclear changes but none of them could be *made* to release this energy, as can happen in certain chemical reactions when two substances react.

The discovery that the release of nuclear energy can be brought about intentionally on a large scale was made by German physicists Otto Hahn and Fritz Strassman in Berlin in 1938. They knew that nuclei bombarded by neutrons might become unstable and release more neutrons which could cause more nuclei to become unstable. Their search for a suitable type of nucleus that behaved in this way was rewarded when they discovered that a uranium 235 nucleus (a form of uranium with three fewer neutrons per nucleus than uranium 238, the much more abundant form of uranium) splits into two when it is bombarded by neutrons. The process is called 'fission', and Hahn and Strassman discovered that it releases much more energy than is released in a chemical reaction. Hahn wrote urgently to the Austrian nuclear physicist Lise Meitner (1878–1968) who had worked with him on the problem in Berlin, before she was forced to move to Sweden to escape from the Nazi government in Germany. Meitner realized the implications of this discovery and contacted Niels Bohr in Holland who took the news directly to a conference in America. Within days, Hahn and Strassmann's experiment was confirmed and within a few weeks, Irene Joliot Curie in Paris discovered that neutrons are released as well as energy when uranium 235 nuclei are bombarded with neutrons. It became clear that a sufficient mass of uranium 235, little more than a few kilogrammes, would undergo a chain reaction and release a colossal amount of energy in a very short time as a result. Governments in several countries realized the importance of these discoveries and teams of scientists in Britain, Germany and America set to work on secret projects which only became known to the public when the first atomic bombs were dropped on the Japanese cities of Nagasaki and Hiroshima in 1945, bringing World War II to a rapid end.

EINSTEIN AND THE BOMB

Einstein left Germany in December 1932 and never returned, aware that if he did he would not escape persecution at the hands of the Nazi government which had taken over the country in early 1933. He used his influence on tour in Britain and America to urge support for organizations providing refuge for the many Jewish scientists and other intellectuals in Germany dismissed and dispossessed by the Nazi government. Einstein was settled in America at Princeton, and it was here that he heard about the work of Hahn, Strassmann and Joliot Curie. He realized that a uranium bomb could be made and that this would have a devastating effect if dropped on a city and its inhabitants. In a letter to President Roosevelt in 1939, he urged the US government to make such a bomb before the Nazi government did. He knew that the Nazis would not hesitate to use it if their enemies did not possess such a weapon to use in retaliation. In fact, Einstein did not need to urge such a course of action, as scientists in Britain and America had already been set to work by their governments. In Princeton, Einstein carried on with his theoretical research on gravity and the quantum theory, unaware that experiments on nuclear fission were being conducted nearby and in other research centres in America and Britain.

✳ ✳ ✳ ✳ SUMMARY ✳ ✳ ✳ ✳

- Mass is a mesure of how much matter is present in an object.

- Energy is the capacity of a body to do work.

- The energy E of an object and its mass m are related by the equation $E = mc^2$, where c is the speed of light in free space.

- The mass m of an object increases with its speed γ in accordance with the equation $m = \gamma \, m_0$, where the Lorentz factor $\gamma = m_0/(1 - v^2/c^2)^{-1/2}$ and m_0 is the rest mass.

- No object (other than a photon) can travel as fast as light. The mass of an object tends to infinity as its speed approches the speed of light.

The Challenge of Gravity 5

After Einstein was appointed to a full-time professorship in Zurich in 1909, he was able to spend all his time and energy developing his ideas about relativity. The ideas that we have met so far gave Einstein a respected position among the leading scientists of the age. He wanted to generalize his 1905 theory of relativity to find a general theory that would enable the laws of physics to be expressed in the same form in all frames of reference, not just in inertial frames of reference (see page 19). In his 1905 theory, he had shown how to transform the equations of mechanics and of electromagnetic waves from one inertial frame of reference to another so the equations remained unchanged. His struggle to show how this can be done for any frame of reference took over a decade and his successful prediction of the bending of starlight grazing the Sun during an eclipse was to bring him worldwide fame as the man who created a totally new perception of space, time and gravity.

Further evidence to support Einstein's General Theory of Relativity has been found in more recent experiments involving radar and space probes and in astronomical observations of double images of distant galaxies and black holes. Such support boosts the credibility of other predictions derived from the work on gravity by Einstein and others, notably the Big Bang Theory of the origin of the Universe. We will look at these further experiments and predictions later in this book. In this chapter and the next, we will concentrate on Einstein's ideas about gravity.

GRAVITY RULES

Before Newton established his theory of gravity, it was thought that objects rose into the air due to a property called 'levity' and then fell due to gravity. Newton was born in 1642, the same year that Galileo died, in the market town of Grantham in east England. His father died before he was born and he was brought up by a grandparent after his mother remarried. He was sent to the local grammar school as a boarder and entered Cambridge University in 1661. England at this time was a republic under Oliver Cromwell. The university was closed at times during 1665 and 1666 because of the Great Plague which was ravaging the country. Newton returned home and in just two years produced mathematical theorems and physical theories, including his law of gravitation, that revolutionized mathematics and physics. This quiet period in Newton's life proved to be his most productive years, not unlike Einstein's years in Berne when undemanding work at the Patent Office allowed him to develop the Theory of Special Relativity. He returned to Cambridge in 1667 and was appointed two years later at 26 years of age to the Chair of Mathematics at Trinity College.

A likely story

After Newton had put forward his theory of gravity, a tale began to circulate of how his thoughts on gravity originated when an apple fell on his head as he was sitting under a tree in summer at home. Regardless of the authenticity of the tale, it conjures up a memorable picture of an object being attracted by the force of gravity due to the Earth. However, it leaves out the fact that there is an equal and opposite force on the Earth due to the apple and neglects the question of how the force of gravity acts between two objects.

Newton showed that a force of gravitational attraction exists between any two objects. He explained the motion of an object falling to the ground by saying that the object and the Earth attract each other. He used the same idea to explain why the Moon goes round the Earth and why the planets go round the Sun. If the force of gravity between the Sun and the planets suddenly ceased to exist, each planet would continue in uniform motion in a straight line at a tangent to its orbit. The force of gravitational attraction between the planet and the Sun keeps

Figure 4: Gravity at work

the planet circling the Sun. Newton thought that the force of gravity
between two objects was proportional to:

* the mass of each object;

* the inverse of the square of the distance between the two objects,
  provided this distance is much greater than the size of the objects.

For two such objects of masses m_1 and m_2 at distance apart r, Newton
formed the following equation for the force of gravity F between the
two masses:

$$F = G \frac{m_1 \, m_2}{r^2}$$

where G is a constant which he referred to as the Universal Constant of
Gravitation.

Newton's choice of r^2 in his equation rather than r or r^3 or some other power of r was inspired by his previous discoveries of the laws of motion. He knew that an object accelerated when it was acted on by a force and he had worked out that a body in steady circular motion always experienced an acceleration towards the centre of the circle. He had worked out that this acceleration was equal to the (speed)^2/radius. By linking this to his force formula, he proved Kepler's third law of planetary motion, namely that the cube of the mean radius of the orbit of a planet about the Sun is in proportion to the square of the time it takes to go round the Sun once. This law was established by the Prague astronomer, Johannes Kepler (1571–1630), early in the seventeenth century. Newton had to use r^2 rather than any other power of r in his force formula in order to prove Kepler's third law. Newton's law of gravity with its 'inverse square relationship' linking the force of gravity between two objects to their separation successfully explains many astronomical observations and events, including the motion of the planets and comets round the Sun, of moons round the planets, of satellites round the Earth, and of the tides on the Earth. It is used to predict tides, eclipses, comet and satellite orbits, planetary positions, escape speeds from planets, planetary atmospheres and many other astronomical and planetary features. Over two centuries later, Einstein was to use another set of astronomical measurements to overturn Newton's ideas on gravity.

THE PRINCIPLE OF EQUIVALENCE

Science can be very entertaining, as Galileo reportedly showed in Pisa when he demonstrated that falling objects released from the top of the Leaning Tower of Pisa hit the ground at the same time. He concluded that the acceleration of a falling object is independent of its weight. Even today, this finding comes as a surprise to many people, generally as a result of imagining that a heavy object ought to descend at a faster rate than a lighter object because the force of gravity on the heavier object is greater. Newton provided the explanation when he asserted that the acceleration of any object acted on by a force is:

* proportional to the force on the object;
* inversely proportional to the mass of the object.

For example, the acceleration of a truck from standstill will be reduced if the truck is carrying a heavy load even though the engine force is the same. In the case of a falling object, the acceleration is unaffected by the mass. For example, if the mass is doubled, the force of gravity is also doubled but this increased force acts on double the mass so the acceleration is unchanged. The increase in the force of gravity on a larger mass in free fall has no effect on the acceleration because the force is acting on an increased mass.

ACTIVITY

Drop two different-sized coins at the same time from the same height above a level floor. The two coins should hit the floor simultaneously. The sound of the impacts are heard as a single sound only.

Einstein had already worked out in the Theory of Special Relativity that mass increases with speed. He realized that the mass of an object has two fundamental properties, namely that it determines the force of gravity on the object and also determines its resistance to changing its motion, a property known as inertia.

Two objects that experience equal forces of gravity must have equal masses. If the force of gravity on one object is ten times the force of gravity on another object, the masses of the two objects must be in the ratio ten to one. The mass of one object can be compared with the mass of another object using a weighing machine. If the two objects have equal weights, they must have equal masses.

Inertia is a measure of the difficulty of causing change, in this case changing the velocity of an object. A massive tanker at sea has a huge amount of inertia and takes several kilometres to stop because it has a very large mass. The same would apply to a rocket in space, well beyond the force of gravity of the Earth or any other body. Changing the velocity of an object is more difficult the larger the mass of the object is. Another method of comparing the masses of two objects is to compare how they respond in terms of inertia to the same force. For example, the more massive an object is, the longer it takes to reach a certain speed from rest when a certain 'inertial' force acts on it. If two objects have the same mass, they should take the same duration to reach the same speed when acted on by the same force.

The masses of two objects can therefore be compared by weighing them or by comparing their inertial response to the same force. If the mass of one of the objects is known, the mass of the other object can be determined by each method. The gravitational mass (i.e. mass measured by the weighing method) should be equal to the inertial mass (i.e. the mass measured by changing its velocity). This equality of the gravitational mass and the inertial mass of an object is the reason why falling objects descend at the same rate, as Galileo discovered. The test has been repeated by different experiments using different methods in recent times using rather more sophisticated equipment to give the same outcome to an astonishing degree of accuracy of less than 1 part in 100 million. The overall conclusion is that the ratio of the gravitational mass of an object to its inertial mass is the same for any object.

Since gravitational mass seems to be the same as inertial mass, is it possible to distinguish between gravity and accelerated or decelerated motion? In Chapter 3, we saw that it is not possible to distinguish between being in a state of rest and moving at constant speed without change of direction. What about distinguishing between gravity and changing motion? Einstein thought very deeply about the link between gravity and accelerated motion. A person floating about in a windowless capsule would not know if the capsule was in a gravity-free environment far away from the Earth or in free-fall above the Earth – until the capsule hit the ground! Einstein came to the conclusion that the effects of gravity and accelerated motion are identical and are in effect indistinguishable. On this basis, known as the **Principle of Equivalence**, he developed his ideas that led to the General Theory of Relativity in which he proved that a gravitational field causes space and time to be distorted. Einstein's papers on the Principle of Equivalence were published in 1907 and 1908 when he was still a full-time employee of the Berne Patent Office.

> **KEYWORD**
>
> Principle of Equivalence: this asserts that the effects of gravity and of accelerated motion are identical.

* Weight is the pull of gravity on an object.
* Inertia is the resistance of an object to change of its motion.
* The effects of gravity and accelerated motion are indistinguishable.

Over the next few years, Einstein thought about the effect of gravity on light, reasoning that a photon of energy $E = hf$ possesses a mass $m = hf/c^2$ in accordance with $E = mc^2$ even though the speed of a photon is always c and it has no rest mass. Thus it seemed to Einstein that photons would be affected by gravity, just as other objects are. He published his ideas about gravity and light in 1911, predicting not only the deflection of light by gravity but also the change of energy of a light photon passing in or out of a gravitational field. We will look in more detail in Chapter 6 about his ideas on gravity and light, and how it led him to conclude that space and time are distorted by gravity.

* * * *SUMMARY* * * *

* Newton's theory of gravity: any two point objects exert a force of gravitational attraction on each other which is proportional to the masses of the objects and inversely proportional to their distance apart.

* The Principle of Equivalence: the effects of gravity and accelerated motion are indistinguishable.

6 Towards General Relativity

Einstein had been a full-time researcher in physics for just two years when, in 1911, he was invited to the 1st Solvay Congress in Brussels. This was organized by the Belgian industrialist, Ernest Solvay with the intention of bringing Europe's leading physicists together to discuss the profound developments in the subject over the past two decades. Einstein delivered a paper on the thermal properties of materials at low temperatures, impressing those present with his clarity and depth of knowledge. Yet his thoughts as a researcher had moved on to much deeper territory to do with gravity in an intellectual struggle which preoccupied him until 1916 when he published his General Theory of Relativity. His Principle of Equivalence had led him to think about the effect of gravity on light, which had led him to the realization that the shortest distance between two points in a gravitational field is not a straight line, and to the idea that space is not necessarily flat. From this, he worked out the exact effect of the Sun's gravity on starlight skimming its surface.

GRAVITY AND LIGHT

Light travels on a straight path – unless it passes through a strong gravitational field. We will look at the actual experimental evidence that gravity bends light later in this chapter. Einstein worked out how much a light beam passing near the Sun should be bent by the Sun's gravity. His calculations were based on very complicated mathematics, although the essential idea is not too complicated if we start by thinking about a light beam passing through opposite-facing portholes of an accelerating rocket.

If the path of the beam could be made visible to an observer in the rocket, perhaps by making the beam skim across a screen, the observer would see a curved path like the path of a stone thrown sideways from the top of a tower. The acceleration of the rocket causes the observer to see a curved light path. As acceleration cannot be distinguished from gravity, it therefore follows that gravity should cause a light beam to curve too.

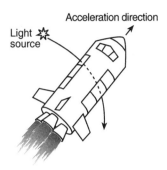

Figure 5: Light bending in an accelerating rocket

Einstein had already established that light consists of 'photons' which are massless packets of
electromagnetic energy equal to hf (see page
41). He had also shown that energy and mass
are linked by the equation $E = mc^2$. His initial
approach to the problem was to imagine that
light photons skimming past the Sun's surface
would be deflected by the Sun's gravity in

KEYWORD

Deflection of a light
beam: the angle it is
turned through; the angle
is measured in seconds of
arc where 3600 seconds
of arc = 1 degree.

much the same way as a high-speed rocket skimming past the Moon
would be deflected. In 1911, he showed that the **deflection of a light
beam** skimming the edge of the Sun should be $2GM/Rc^2$, which gives
about 0.9 seconds of arc, equivalent to the angle between the lines to
your eye from opposite edges of a small coin about 2 km away.

AN UNSUCCESSFUL MISSION

To test whether or not light is deflected by gravity, Einstein accepted an
offer from Erwin Freundlich, a young astronomer at the University of
Berlin, to photograph the total solar eclipse of 1914 in southern Russia.
The Sun would be blocked out by the Moon, enabling stars in the
Hyades star cluster to be seen very close to the eclipsed Sun. If the Sun's
gravity affected light, then these stars would be seen slightly further
from the Sun than they would be if their light was unaffected by the
Sun. Accurate measurements on these photographs would enable the

question to be settled. Sponsors were found to finance the expedition and by summer 1914, Freundlich and his team were in place for the event. Unfortunately, Germany declared war on Russia on 1 August 1914 and the expedition team was arrested and returned to Berlin without their equipment.

Perhaps this failure was fortunate for Einstein as he had to wait until 1919 before another test could be made, giving him time to develop his ideas about gravity as he realized the need to describe space and time using the mathematics of curved surfaces developed by Georg Riemann in 1854. By 1913, he had developed an outline of what was to become the General Theory of Relativity. The essence of his approach was to develop a mathematical theory relating points in space and time by means of equations which are the same for any frame of reference, accelerating or not, taking gravity into account. In 1916 he predicted correctly from the General Theory of Relativity that the deflection is $4GM/Rc^2$, twice his prediction of 1911. If Freundlich had been successful in 1914, Einstein's 1911 theory might have been dismissed and the 1916 theory might not have emerged.

EINSTEIN'S RETURN JOURNEY

Ever since he had been a student at the ETH, Einstein had been much influenced by the philosophical views of Ernst Mach, a physicist who was reaching the end of a long, prestigious career just as Einstein was achieving recognition in the scientific world. Mach held the view that observations and experiments should guide us to discover the nature of the physical world. He disapproved of concepts such as absolute space and time that cannot be defined by experience. In 1911, Einstein moved from Zurich to Prague to take up the post of a full professor of physics at the German University of Prague, attracted by the higher salary and better facilities at a major European university where Mach had been the Rector many years before.

Zurich had suited Einstein and his wife, Mileva, and two children. He enjoyed sailing and walking and talking about physics with his students in the local café. Einstein found his new duties at his post in Prague involved experimental physics, which he disliked, and he was also expected to undertake administrative duties. His unease became known to colleagues in Zurich and, within a little over a year, he was back in Zurich as Professor of Mathematical Physics at the ETH. Back in Zurich, Einstein worked with Marcel Grossman, one of his friends from his student days at ETH, starting the development of the mathematical methods that were to lead to the General Theory of Relativity. Einstein's reputation as a theoretical physicist flourished back in Zurich, and his lectures and meetings were usually crowded. Eminent scientists visited him in Zurich and he was persuaded by Planck to move with his family from Zurich to Berlin in April 1914 to become director of the Kaiser Wilhelm Institute for Physics, a research institution created for Einstein so he could carry on his research without other distracting duties, at the same time keeping in close contact with other eminent physicists in Berlin such as Planck. When war broke out in August that year, his wife and two sons returned to Zurich but Einstein, by that stage immersed in his research, did not follow. His first marriage ended in divorce some years later.

THE PERIHELION PROBLEM

By 1915, Einstein's work had developed sufficiently to provide an explanation of a problem concerning the **elliptical orbit** of the planet Mercury. This problem had worried astronomers for many decades ever since the 1840s, when astronomers had used their measurements to show that the **perihelion** of Mercury's orbit, its closest approach to the Sun, advances at a rate of 0.159 degrees (equivalent to 574 seconds of arc) per century. In 1859, Urbain Le Verrier, a French mathematician, used Newton's theory of gravity to work out that most of this advance could be explained by the effect of the other planets on Mercury. However, he was unable to account for 43 seconds of arc and, for half a century, nor could any one else – until Einstein!

KEYWORDS

Elliptical orbit: a non-circular orbit in the shape of an ellipse.

Perihelion: the point of closest approach of a planet or comet to the Sun.

Using his developing General Theory of Relativity, Einstein proved that an advance of the perihelion in the absence of any other planet was to be expected. He derived a formula for the expected advance per orbit and used it to calculate that Mercury's perihelion ought to advance at a rate of 43 seconds of arc per century – exactly the amount that Le Verrier in 1859 had been unable to account for. Astronomers had searched without success for the existence of another planet, even giving it the name Vulcan, supposing it to be tugging on Mercury from an orbit closer to the Sun. Their failure to find an acceptable cause within the framework of Newton's theory of gravity worried them. Einstein was able to explain why this perihelion advance occurs and he used his theory to calculate the rate of advance at the observed value. He presented his explanation in autumn 1915 at the Prussian Academy of Sciences.

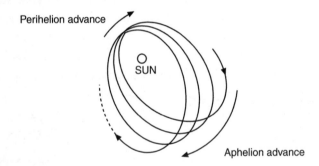

Figure 6: Mercury's advancing perihelion

By summer 1916, he had completed the General Theory of Relativity, having used the theory to work out that a light beam that passes near the edge of the Sun should be deflected by an angle of 1.75 seconds of arc, twice the angle predicted by his simpler 1911 theory He proved that the angle of deflection is equal to $4GM/Rc^2$, where M is the mass of the Sun, R is its radius, G is the universal constant of gravitation and c is the speed of light.

ACROSS ENEMY LINES

Einstein sent a copy of his General Theory of Relativity, via Willem de Sitter, Professor of Astronomy at the University of Leiden in Holland, to the secretary of the Royal Astronomical Society, Arthur Eddington, in London. Eddington was also Professor of Astronomy at Cambridge and a top-class mathematician who realized the significance of Einstein's theory immediately. He published the theory in the society's monthly notices and persuaded Sir Frank Dyson, the Astronomer Royal, to arrange a study (which proved inconclusive) of photographs of the 1905 eclipse. Although Britain and Germany were at war, Dyson and Eddington realized the enormous significance of Einstein's theory if it could be verified and they made plans to use the 1919 solar eclipse to test Einstein's prediction. The armies of the British Empire were suffering huge casualties on the Western Front, Britain was under a tightening U-boat blockade, the Russian front was collapsing and America's entry to the war was not yet certain. Dyson and Eddington knew that Einstein was not in favour of war between nations and had little time for the military ambitions of the German government. He was a Swiss citizen who had only accepted German nationality to work with top physicists such as Planck in Berlin. His pacifist views were to change however after World War I as anti-Semitism in Germany grew, forcing him to emigrate to America in 1932.

After publishing the General Theory of Relativity in 1916, Einstein started working through the consequences of his theory. In 1917, he published a paper on its cosmological consequences which rekindled interest in the subject among fellow scientists and astronomers. We will look at these consequences later in this book. Einstein's work on relativity over more than a decade had provided scientists with a completely new framework to think about, almost beyond the imagination of any other scientist at the start of the decade. By 1916, he was clearly one of the most outstanding scientists of his generation. Even if the General Theory of Relativity had proved a failure, his place as a key twentieth-century scientist alongside Planck, the originator of the quantum theory, and Rutherford, the father of nuclear physics, was assured because of his work on Special Relativity. In fact, his General Theory of Relativity was to establish his reputation even beyond that of Newton two centuries earlier.

 **✻ ✻ ✻ ✻SUMMARY ✻ ✻ ✻ ✻**

- Perihelion advance of Mercury explained by Einstein in 1915.

- General Theory of Relativity published by Einstein in 1916, including the prediction that light grazing the Sun is deflected by an angle of 1.75 arc seconds.

7 A Journey into Space-Time

After publishing his Special Theory of Relativity in 1905, Einstein worked on his ideas linking gravity, space and time until he was able to publish his General Theory of Relativity in 1916. Much of his work involved very complicated mathematical methods which he combined with insight and intuition that took him well beyond the level at which any of his contempories were working. Just as Newton over two centuries earlier had taken mathematics and physics forward in great leaps, Einstein was to do likewise to produce a theory whose predictions were completely unexpected and totally beyond the visions of any other scientist or mathematician since Newton. We will look later at the experimental evidence to date that supports the General Theory of Relativity. For the moment, however, let's look briefly at how the theory emerged and what mathematical ideas underpin it.

COORDINATES AND MAPS

In the Special Theory of Relativity, Einstein had shown that space and time are not absolute quantities, and he derived the equations explained in Chapter 3 that relate observations made by a stationary observer to those made by an observer moving at constant velocity. In effect, his special relativity equations enable the laws of physics, such as conservation of energy, to be valid in all frames of reference moving at

constant velocity relative to each other. The next stage was to prove the general principle of relativity, namely that the laws of physics are the same for all observers Between 1905–1916, Einstein worked on trying to show the laws of physics are the same in an **accelerated frame of reference**. He recognized the significance of the link between accelerated motion and gravity, and went on to show how gravity affects space and time.

Figure 7: Flat space

To appreciate some of Einstein's work, a good place to start such a journey is by looking at a map of your home country on a flat table. Suppose you want to work out the direct distance between your home and another location on the map that is 50 km north and 80 km. The direct distance can be worked out using Pythagoras' theorem, as in Figure 8.

The direct distance s is therefore given by the equation, $s^2 = x^2 + y^2$ where x = 80 km and y = 50 km. The distances x and y are like map coordinates and tell you the how far north or south and how far east or west one point is from another. In this case: $s^2 = 80^2 + 50^2 = 8900$ so $s = \sqrt{8900} = 94$ km

Now suppose you want to find the direct distance along the surface between two points on a globe of the Earth. Pythagoras' theorem won't work on this scale because the distance is not insignificant compared with the Earth's radius. Einstein knew from the work of mathematicians such as Karl Friedrich Gauss (1777–1855) that the distance, δs between any two nearby points on a curved surface can be expressed in a general form:

$$\delta s^2 = g_{11}\,\delta x_1{}^2 + g_{12}\,\delta x_1\,\delta x_2 + g_{22}\,\delta x_2{}^2$$

where δ signifies a small distance and x_1 and x_2 are the two coordinates of any point on the surface, for example the distance along the equator and the distance north or south of the equator. Each of the quantities g_{11}, g_{12} and g_{22} changes its value with position because the surface is curved not flat.

Gauss and the triangle rule

It's a well-known fact that the angles of a triangle add up to 180°. In fact, this is only true if the triangle is flat. To make a flat triangle, all you need to do is to draw straight lines between three dots on a piece of paper. The straight line joining any two of the dots of the triangle is the shortest possible line between those two dots. If you make three dots on a ball and join the dots, you finish up with a triangle that is not flat and for which the angles do not add up to 180°, even if you make the lines as short as possible. Gauss used surveying instruments to measure the angles of a very big triangle formed by three mountain tops. He wanted to see if the angles added up to 180° because he thought space might not be flat on such a large scale. Perhaps he was disappointed to find that the angles did add up to 180°. He had no evidence that space was not flat.

CURVED SURFACES

A surface consists of points that are linked by some condition. For example, a horizontal table top is a surface of constant height. The condition linking the points of a surface can be expressed by means of a mathematical equation. The equation for a horizontal table top is 'height = constant'. A sphere is a surface that has the same curvature everywhere as its radius R is constant. You can draw many circles of different radii on the surface of a sphere. The shortest distance between any two points on a sphere is a line which is part of a circle of radius equal to the radius of the sphere. A rugby ball has a surface that has a curvature that changes with position. The curvature is greatest at the ends and least midway between the ends.

A cylinder has a surface that is flat in one direction and has a constant curvature at right angles to its flat direction. Imagine a playground shaped like part of the surface of a cylinder with two points marked on it at opposite corners. What is the shortest path from one corner to the other? One way to find out would be to count the steps needed to go from one corner to the other for different routes. The shortest path would have the least number of steps. A mathematical way to do this was discovered by Georg Riemann, a German mathematician who developed Gauss's ideas and found out how to express the curvature of a surface in terms of any system of coordinates. His generalized approach involved combinations of gradients in different directions. He went on to show how to find the shortest route between two points on a surface. In 1912, Einstein started to use Riemann's methods to find the path of light in a gravitational field but he became discouraged by the formidable mathematical methods involved, in spite of help from Marcel Grossman, when he returned to Zurich. He sought a different approach after 1913 but made little progress so he returned to Riemann's geometry in 1915 and his persistence was rewarded within a year.

How to measure curvature

A curve is a line with a gradient or steepness that changes along the line. To measure the curvature at a point on a line, imagine a magnified view of the line at this point. Draw a straight line at right angles to the curve through the point. Repeat the procedure for a nearby point. The two straight lines intersect at the centre of curvature of the section of the line between the two points. This section forms part of a circle centred on the centre of curvature. The radius of curvature, r, is the radius of this circle. The curvature is defined as $1/r^2$. The larger the circle, the smaller its curvature. A straight line has no curvature. Riemann worked out a formula to find the curvature of a line on surface, given the defining equation for the surface.

Figure 8: Prospecting

SPACE-TIME

An event in space and time is defined by three spatial coordinates (x_1, x_2 and x_3) and a fourth coordinate, which we will label x_4, which represents the distance travelled by light in a specified time. The coordinates are measured from an original event at $x_1 = x_2 = x_3 = x_4 = 0$. The formula for the interval δs (see page 49) can be extended to any two nearby events or points in space and time to give the following equation, which is known as the metric in which g_{ij} is referred to as the metric tensor:

$$\delta s^2 = g_{ij}\, \delta x_i\, \delta x_j$$

where i and j run through all the possible combinations of 1, 2, 3 and 4.

Because of the way the coordinates are combined in the metric, it isn't possible to separate them generally into space coordinates and time coordinates. For this reason, the term 'space-time' is used rather than 'space and time'. The position and motion of a particle can be represented by a line through space time. The quantity represents δs the interval between two points in space-time. This quantity is invariant, (the same, regardless of the system of coordinates chosen). For example, the distance between two points on the Earth's surface is an invariant as it is the same regardless of the coordinate system chosen.

In general, the metric tensor, g_{ij}, varies with position, in the same way that the strength of the Earth's magnetic field does. In effect, it represents a 'weighting factor' as to how much each pair of coordinate elements δx_i δx_j contributes to δs^2. A tensor is any quantity consisting of components calculated from the coordinates that transform from one coordinate system into any other coordinate system in the same way as the coordinate elements do.

Einstein worked out that there are certain other tensors derived from the metric tensor that can represent quantities other than the interval δs that are invariant. These other tensors are complicated combinations of the metric tensor and derivatives from it in the form of its gradients and the rates of changes of the gradients in different directions. The quantities they represent are unchanged in any transformation from one coordinate system to another. By expressing the laws of physics in the form of such tensors, Einstein was able to show that the laws are independent of the coordinate system used to describe them. In particular, he discovered that tensor methods produce Newton's law of gravitation for weak gravity. Encouraged by this discovery, Einstein considered what would happen if gravity was not quite as weak and he found that if his proof of Newton's law of gravitation was applied to the empty space near a sufficiently large central mass, an extra term appeared which affected the motion of a smaller body in orbit about the large central mass. As outlined on page 44, he used this extra term to explain the problem of the perihelion advance of the planet Mercury which Newton's theory could not explain and which had puzzled astronomers since 1859.

BEYOND DOUBT

Rather than believe Einstein's extremely complicated mathematical theory, many scientists preferred to believe that the discrepancy could be on account of an undiscovered planet closer to the Sun tugging on Mercury. Einstein was undaunted by the doubters and he gained support from the German astronomer Karl Schwarzschild (1873–1916) who presented Einstein's theory in a clearer form. Einstein developed Schwarzschild's approach further and so discovered an important tensor which became known as the Einstein tensor, E_{ij} (see Appendix 2). This represents the difference between the curvature in a certain direction along a certain line at a given point and the local curvature at that point after taking the 'weighting factor' for directions into account. Einstein then deduced how this tensor depends on the distribution of mass and energy in space time. He published these discoveries and his predictions as the General Theory of Relativity in 1916, founded on the principle that all frames of reference are equally valid, and that the laws of physics should be the same in any frame of reference.

Figure 9: Twists and turns

Time for a walk

Imagine a footpath that winds round and up a hill. The gradient of the footpath along the footpath is its steepness and its gradient across the footpath is its inclination. Great care would be needed where the outer edge of the path is below the inside edge, especially if the footpath is steep as well. The curvature of the footpath is a measure of how it twists and turns, in terms of its changing steepness and inclination. Imagine the path is like a very long roll of wallpaper twisting and turning as it winds up the hillside. The curvature at any point on the footpath can be measured in terms of:

* the change of its steepness along its length (i.e. how much it curves along its length);

* the change of its steepness across its width (i.e. how much it twists across its width);

* the change of its inclination along its length (i.e. how much it twists along its length);

* the change of its inclination across its width (i.e. how much it curves across its width).

The local curvature at a point is the average of the above four measures. In essence, the Einstein tensor consists of components that each represent the difference between each of the above measures of curvature and the local curvature. In simple terms, it describes the local distortions of space-time. See also Appendix 2 for further explanation.

CURVATURE AND STRESS

In his theory, Einstein used E_{ij} to relate the distortion of space-time to the distribution and motion of matter and radiation in space-time, to form a general equation which may be expressed as:

distortion of space time = constant x energy distribution

* The distortion is represented by the Einstein tensor E_{ij} which corresponds to the variation of curvature in the direction of the x_i coordinate axis along the line of the x_j coordinate axis.

❋ The distribution is expressed through a further tensor, the mass-energy tensor T_{ij}, which represents the stress or pressure due to the concentration of energy in space-time. The greater the energy density in a small region, the larger the stress acting at the boundaries of the region. In effect, T_{ij} is a measure of the stress at a point in the direction of the x_i coordinate axis acting on a small area perpendicular to the x_j coordinate axis.

Thus the above equation may be thought of as showing that the change of curvature in a certain direction along a certain line is in proportion to the stress in that direction along the same line. By choosing the constant as $-8\pi G/c^2$, Einstein found he was able to show that the equation reduced to Newton's Law of Gravitation (see page 35) for weak gravity.

The general equation means that the distribution of matter and energy in space time determines the curvature of space time, which determines the motion of matter and energy. Instead of the Newtonian conception of matter and energy existing in absolute space and time, the equation above means that the distribution of matter and energy determines space time, which determines the motion of matter and energy.

Predictions

Einstein made two important predictions from the General Theory of Relativity about the effect of gravity on light.

1 The energy and hence frequency of a photon escaping from a gravitational field changes. This prediction could not be tested at the time but has since been confirmed, as explained on page 62. However, since then, other theories too have been used to explain this effect.

2 Light grazing the Sun is deflected by 1.75 seconds of arc. The success of Einstein's explanation of the perihelion advance of Mercury's orbit led Eddington to plan an expedition to South America to observe the total solar eclipse of 1919 in order to measure the shift of position of stars near the edge of the solar disc during a total solar eclipse. The result confirmed Einstein's prediction, but to an accuracy of no more than about 30%.

UNIVERSAL MEASURES

Einstein found out how to express the laws of physics in a general form which could be transformed to any frame of reference. He also discovered that certain geometrical quantities, such as the local curvature of space-time are invariant (i.e. the same, regardless of the frame of reference) and therefore part of nature. Regardless of the frame of reference used to make appropriate measurements to determine such a quantity, the quantity has the same value at any given point in space-time.

The local curvature of space-time near an object of sufficiently large mass varies from point to point. Imagine a heavy ball placed at the centre of a trampoline. The curvature of the trampoline surface changes with position but it has the same value at a given position, regardless of how it is measured. The path of a marble rolled across the surface without hitting the ball would be deflected, like a photon skimming the Sun. If the marble rolled round the ball on an elliptical path near the ball, it would distort the surface which would cause the point of closest approach to advance. In short, matter curves space-time and space-time moves matter.

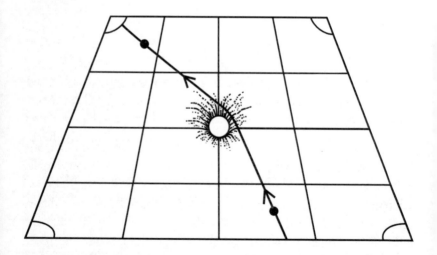

Figure 10: Local distortion

The force of gravity between two objects was thought by Newton to act instantaneously across the distance between the two objects. Einstein showed that two objects attract each other because they affect space-time in between and therefore move towards each other just as two heavy balls released at opposite ends of a trampoline do. He also proved that general relativity becomes special relativity for objects moving at constant velocity, and he showed that general relativity generates Newton's law of gravitation for weak gravity.

Wormholes

Imagine a space probe entering a region where space time is curved by the presence of a massive nearby object. Light would be deflected so distant stars would appear to shift and objects would appear to be distorted. The shortest route between two places would not be along a straight line. A space race would be won by taking advantage of curved space-time although a really ingenious competitor might collect energy from radiation to distort space-time even more – perhaps enough to create a 'wormhole' to tunnel through space-time.

In addition to the predictions outlined earlier, the General Theory of Relativity was used by Einstein and others after its publication to predict the existence of black holes, gravitational lenses, gravitational waves, wormholes and the evolution of the Universe. We will look at the evidence that now supports these predictions and further consequences of Einstein's ideas in the next chapter. No evidence exists as yet for wormholes but they are within the realms of the ideas generated by general relativity.

The success of the eclipse prediction in 1919 forced scientists to accept the General Theory of Relativity and to reject the idea of absolute space and time. No preferred frame of reference exists and no hypothetical substance such as the ether pervading space is needed. Einstein's theory followed logically without any assumptions other than an assertion that the fundamental laws of physics should hold in any frame of reference. Einstein discovered that all the laws of mechanics and electromagnetic radiation could be expressed by the equation $E_{ij} = -\dfrac{8\pi G}{c^2} T_{ij}$.

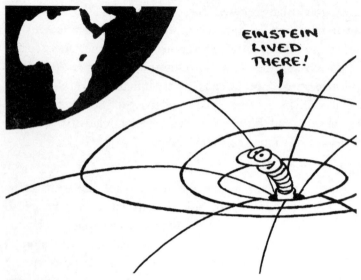

Figure 11: Wormholes

Following the 1919 eclipse and his sudden rise from a leading scientist to a worldwide celebrity, Einstein travelled widely in response to invitations from many countries to deliver lectures. As we shall see in Chapter 11, he continued without success to develop his theory to try to combine quantum theory and general relativity into a unified theory.

✳✳✳✳SUMMARY ✳✳✳✳

- The General Principle of Relativity states that the laws of physics are the same for all observers.

- The General Theory of Relativity is the mathematical theory devised by Einstein to prove the General Principle of Relativity. Einstein showed that space-time is distorted by the distribution of matter and energy in accordance with the equation: **distortion = constant x energy distribution.**

- Predictions made by Einstein include:

1 the gravitional red shift of a photon escaping from a gravitational field;

2 the deflection of light grazing the Sun.

New Discoveries 8

More predictions and new discoveries followed from Einstein's General Theory of Relativity, including some in recent decades as a result of better technology in astronomy. The same process had happened after Newton had established his theory of gravitation. The discovery of the outer planet Neptune was made as a result of investigating differences between the observed motion of the planet Uranus and its predicted motion according to Newton's law. Astronomers before Newton reckoned there might be more planets and Newton's theory provided the information on where to search for them in the night sky. However, the predictions from the General Theory of Relativity that have been confirmed would have been mostly beyond imagination without Einstein's discovery. Apart from the idea of black holes, no scientist before Einstein had even considered the possibility of gravitational lenses, gravitational radiation or the theory of the Big Bang origin of the Universe. In this chapter, we will look at some of the evidence now available that supports these predictions.

DOUBLE IMAGES IN SPACE

Until recent decades convincing evidence for the General Theory of Relativity rested only on the deflection of light near the Sun. Between 1968–1978, measurements were made of the transit time of reflected radar pulses sent from Earth to Mercury, Venus to Mars and to the Viking and Mariner space probes. The measurements were made as each object was eclipsed by the Sun and proved to within 0.1% that the deflection was 1.75 seconds of arc. There is now little doubt that space is curved near the Sun and the curvature is as predicted by Einstein.

If gravity bends light, is it possible to make gravity form images? A magnifying glass is a glass lens that makes objects appear larger. It does this by changing the direction of light passing through it, making the light appear to have come from an enlarged image.

A straight-sided glass of water can act as a magnifying glass too. Look at a coin through a glass of water and you will see a magnified image of the coin (the image will probably be distorted if the coin is very close to the glass). You might even see an extra image at each edge of the glass, as well as the central image. The extra images are formed because light from the coin travelling to the edges of the glass is bent by the combined effect of the water and the glass, as shown in Figure 12. This raises the question can gravity cause distorted images of objects in space?

Figure 12: Light bending to form a double image

In 1979, astronomers found the first direct evidence of a double image in space when they discovered a double **quasar** Q0957 and 561. A quasar is a distant star-like object which emits as much light as an entire galaxy of stars. Quasars are known to be much smaller in diameter than galaxies because light variations from a quasar are of the order of days rather than years, implying that a quasar is a light source that has a diameter of the order of the

KEYWORD

Quasar: acronym for a quasi-stellar object – an object emitting much more light than a star, but that is not much larger in size than a star (the prefix 'quasi' means 'seemingly but not actually', hence 'quasi-skellar' means 'seemingly like a star but not actually a star.

distance travelled by light in days rather than many years. The first quasar was discovered in 1962 and many more have been discovered since. The significance of the 1979 discovery was that the light from each half of the double image fluctuated the same which cannot happen from two quasars as the fluctuations are random. Astronomers realized that they had observed two images of a single quasar hidden by a large mass somewhere between the quasar and the Milky Way, our home galaxy. We see the quasar because its light skimming the edge of the mass is bent round, just as light from the coin in Figure 12 is bent round each edge of the glass. More recently, the Hubble space telescope has revealed images of faint galaxies distorted and spread out into streaks behind clusters of galaxies which act as enormous gravitational lenses. These colourful images leave no doubt that space-time is curved by the presence of mass.

GRAVITATIONAL RED SHIFT

If light is bent by gravity, does its energy change when it enters or leaves a gravitational field? An object thrown into the air loses speed as it rises and therefore loses kinetic energy. What about light directed upwards? Light consists of photons which are wavepackets of electromagnetic energy. The energy of a photon is in proportion to its frequency. According to Einstein's theory, the energy of a photon ought to decrease if it moves up because it uses some of its energy to overcome gravity. This decrease

KEYWORD

Red shift: increase in wavelength of light due to the receding motion of the source or escape from a gravitational field. Red light is at the long wavelength end of the visible spectrum, so light from a receding source is said to be 'red shifted' to longer wavelengths.

of energy causes a decrease of frequency which is the same as an increase of wavelength and is referred to as a **red shift**. The increase of wavelength due to a reduction of frequency can be demonstrated by making waves on a pond and observing how they become more spaced out if the frequency at which they are produced is reduced. The term 'red shift' is used because red light is at the low frequency end of the visible spectrum so lowering the frequency of a light photon shifts it to the red end of the visible spectrum away from the blue end.

Einstein's theory predicts that the gravitational red shift for each metre of height gained near the Earth's surface is 100 kHz for a high-energy photon of frequency 10^{21}Hz. This prediction was tested in 1959 at Harvard University by Robert Pound and Glen Rebhka who measured the frequency shift of high-energy photons from a radioactive source as the photons travelled up a 22.5 m tower to a detector at the top of the tower. Their results agreed with Einstein's prediction to within 1%.

However, the success of the gravitational red shift tests in producing observations in agreement with Einstein's predictions is not now reckoned as convincing evidence for general relativity. This is because gravitational red shifts can be explained in terms of the equivalence between gravity and accelerated motion, without the necessity of using general relativity. The fact that general relativity does predict the red shift does not mean that general relativity is the only explanation, unlike gravitational lensing and gravitational radiation which can only be explained by Einstein's theory.

GRAVITATIONAL RADIATION

Einstein predicted that **binary stars** which are stars in orbit about each other, should emit gravitational waves as they orbit each other. If gravity causes space to be curved, the stars in a binary system should create vibrations in the curvature of space. The General Theory of Relativity predicts that these vibrations cause gravitational waves to travel through space at the speed of light. Convincing evidence for such waves was discovered by Russell Hulse and Joseph Taylor in 1974 as a result of searching for radio pulsars, using the Arecibo radio telescope in Puerto Rico. A **pulsar** is a fast-spinning **neutron star** which is extremely dense. The Earth would be no bigger than about 100 km in diameter if it had the same

KEYWORDS

Binary stars: stars that orbit each other.

Neutron star: the nucleus of a hydrogen atom is an single positively charged particle called a proton. The nucleus of every other type of atom is composed of protons and uncharged particles called neutrons. The mass of a neutron is almost the same as that of a proton. A neutron star is composed of neutrons only.

Pulsar: spinning neutron star that emits a beam of radio waves that sweeps around as the star rotates.

density as a neutron star. A neutron star is formed as a result of a supernova explosion which happens to any massive star when it can emit no more light. A pulsar is a spinning neutron star that emits a beam of radio waves as it spins, like a lighthouse emitting a beam of light that sweeps round the horizon. Each time the radio beam from a pulsar sweeps over the Earth, a radio signal pulse is detected.

Hulse and Taylor were using the radio telescope at Arecibo to search for radio pulsars when they discovered a binary pulsar PSR 1913 + 16 which proved to be very unusual. The pulsar itself emits its radio pulses at a constant rate of 59 milliseconds as it and its companion move round each other. Several other binary pulsars had been detected but not one that had an orbit no larger than the Sun and took just eight hours to complete each orbit. The speed of the pulsar in its orbit worked out to be 300 km/s. In such a close orbit, the perihelion (position of least distance apart) advances much faster than Mercury's 43 arc seconds per year. They measured the rate of advance at 4.2 degrees per year and then used Einstein's theory to calculate the combined masses of the two stars to an accuracy of six figures. They confirmed the mass measurement from the effect of gravitational red shift measurements on the arrival time of the pulses.

Even with this stunning success to backup the General Theory of Relativity, PSR 1913 + 16 had one more surprise in store, which ultimately led to Hulse and Taylor receiving the 1993 Nobel prize for physics. For more than four years after their discovery, Hulse and Taylor continued to monitor the pulsar. According to the General Theory of Relativity, the pulsar and its companion are radiating gravitational waves and therefore losing energy and slowing down. The theory predicted that the orbital period should increase at a rate of 75 microseconds per year. In late 1978, they had gathered sufficient evidence to confirm the predicted effect to within an accuracy of 20%. Their achievement topped the celebrations of Einstein's centenary in 1979. By 1983, they had gathered sufficient evidence to confirm Einstein's predictions within an accuracy of 4%.

Einstein used his General Theory of Relativity to predict successfully the effect of gravity on light and the existence of gravitational radiation. These predictions, unlike the gravitational red shift prediction, cannot be explained without Einstein's theory. The successful observation of the bending of star light skimming the Sun during the eclipse of 1919 convinced most scientists of the correctness of Einstein's theory. However, some notable scientists remained unconvinced and opposed Einstein for many years. Little doubt now exists about the validity of the General Theory of Relativity although a scientific theory can never be proved as the possibility of disagreement with some future experiment can never be discounted. What convinced those who opposed Einstein on scientific grounds? Two further predictions made by scientists and mathematicians who developed Einstein's ideas led to evidence that convinced even those deepest in doubt. We will look in detail at these two further predictions in the next two chapters. Even Einstein would have been amazed at the consequences of these two predictions.

＊＊＊＊SUMMARY＊＊＊＊

- The key evidence for the General Theory of Relativity.

1 Solution to the perihelion problem.

2 Deflection of star light skimming the Sun – eclipse prediction confirmed.

3 Gravitational lensing – double images of quasars caused by the deflection of light by gravity.

4 Gravitational radiation – rapidly rotating binary stars found to emit gravitational radiation.

Black Holes

In the previous chapters, we met some very unusual astronomical objects such as supernovae, pulsars and quasars. Now we will look at black holes, which are among the most mysterious objects studied by present-day astronomers. We will look at how the predictions of black holes came about and the observational evidence found in support of black holes. We will also look at some of the rules about black holes that have been worked out by mathematicians.

NO ESCAPE

In the previous section, we saw that light is deflected by a strong gravitational field. In addition, the frequency of a light photon or an atomic clock is affected by gravity. A gravitational field distorts space and time. In his General Theory of Relativity, Einstein showed

> **KEYWORD**
>
> Black hole: a massive object from which no light can escape.

that a gravitational field acts by curving space. One of the most dramatic effects predicted by Einstein's theory is that light cannot escape from an object which creates sufficiently strong gravity. Such an object is referred to as a **black hole**.

These fascinating objects were first predicted by Reverend John Michell in 1783 although he did not invent the name itself. In fact, the term 'black hole' is of much more recent origin, dating from 1968 when it was coined by an Amercian physicist, John Wheeler. Michell knew from Newton's theory of gravitation that an object projected directly upwards would escape from the Earth if its speed exceeded 11 km/s. This speed is referred to as the escape speed from the Earth. The escape speed from the surface of a planet or a star depends on the strength of gravity at the surface. The stronger the gravitational field, the greater the escape speed needs to be. Michell reckoned that if the mass of a planet or star was great enough, not even light travelling at a speed of

300,000 km/s could escape from its surface. Michell even worked out that a star would need to be about five hundred times as large as the Sun to prevent light escaping.

Shortly after Einstein published his General Theory of Relativity, Karl Schwarzschild derived an exact solution to Einstein's equation linking space, time and gravity. In particular, he showed that the component for the distance coordinate from the centre of the massive body of mass M included the factor $\dfrac{1}{1 - 2GM/rc^2)}$

The implication of this factor was immediately obvious to Schwarzschild, Einstein, Eddington and many other scientists. Something very very odd happens at $r = 2GM/c^2$, now known as the **Schwarzschild radius**, because this value of r makes the bottom line of the factor zero, which makes the factor infinitely large. Working out the effect of this factor on an outgoing light ray, it became clear that such a light ray is trapped within a sphere of radius $2GM/c^2$, and this sphere is a horizon that prevents anyone outside seeing events inside. The idea of a black hole became mathematically respectable. Schwarzschild also predicted the existence of a **singularity** at the centre, a point at which anything inside the **event horizon** ends its existence.

He proved that the radius of a black hole, the Schwarzschild radius R, is related to its mass M in accordance with the equation $R = 2GM/c^2$. If the Earth contracted in diameter to become smaller and smaller without loss of mass, it would need to shrink to about 18mm in diameter before it became a black hole. In comparison, a contracting galactic nucleus of a thousand million stars would become a black hole when all the stars fitted into a space no larger than the solar system.

JOURNEY INTO THE UNKNOWN

The Schwarzschild radius defines the event horizon of a black hole. Any object closer than the Schwarzschild radius to the centre of the black hole is trapped forever inside the event horizon. It would be impossible for an outsider to see an object inside the event horizon as no light from the object could pass through the event horizon. The crew of a space ship being pulled towards a black hole might not be aware that they had passed through the event horizon as they would still be able to see light from distant stars. A distant observer, however, would see the spaceship slow down and stop at the event horizon before disappearing from view.

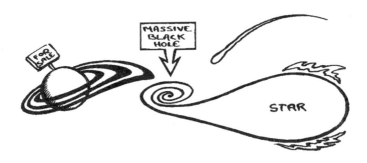

Figure 13: Near a black hole

What happens to the crew of the spaceship once they are inside the black hole? According to Schwarzschild, the spaceship is drawn inexorably towards the centre, to be pulled to shreds by a gravitational field which becomes ever stronger the closer the spacecraft approaches the centre. The spaceship and the crew or their remains would be stretched and stretched more and more as they are pulled into the centre, sucked in like strands of spaghetti. Perhaps this awful fate awaits any inhabitants of planets at the centre of the galaxy where a black hole lurks, feeding on surrounding stars to become heavier and heavier and ever more powerful. Could the Sun and the planets end up in such a cosmic monster?

If nothing can escape from a black hole, it would seem that a black hole is destined to swallow up matter for ever. This prospect conjures up disastrous possibilities but worse is to come in the form of the spinning back hole, dragging space and time round near its event horizon. This was 'discovered' in 1963 by Roy Kerr as an outcome of Einstein's equation when a massive body collapses. Any object near the event horizon would be subjected to a dragging effect due to the rotation of the black hole which could pull it through the event horizon into eternal oblivion. However, an important property of a rotating black hole is that energy can be extracted from it. To do this, an object near the event horizon is broken in two so one part is flung into the black hole against its rotation while the other half is catapulted into space by the rotating motion of the black hole. The first part reduces the black hole's rate of rotation, reducing the energy of the black hole while the second part carries away kinetic energy into space. Perhaps this is part of the mechanism that enables a black hole at the centre of a galaxy to release energy at an enormous rate.

BLACK HOLE RULES

A black hole formed by a massive collapsing star is thought to have no identity other than its mass (which determines its Schwarzschild radius) and its rotation (technically referred to as its angular momentum). A distant external observer cannot tell what object or objects the black hole formed from. This is known by the curious name of the 'no hair' theorem as any attempt to attach anything to a black hole is doomed to failure. Since the surface area of the event horizon of a black hole increases with increased mass, this area is a measure of how much information has been lost through the event horizon. Loss of information creates disorder, which in scientific language is referred to as entropy. Disorder or entropy always increases in any isolated physical process. This is why we can't recover all the energy we obtain from fuel and use it again as it spreads out and makes atoms and molecules more disordered. In the same way, black hole processes in an isolated system create disorder and increase the entropy of the system.

By using analogies with thermodynamics, certain rules for black holes have been developed which make them less likely to create catastrophe. Stephen Hawking at Cambridge has shown that a black hole can actually evaporate as a result of swallowing up **antiparticles** from pairs of particles and antiparticles created near the event horizon. For every known particle, an antiparticle exists with opposite properties such as charge. When an antiparticle meets

KEYWORDS

Antiparticles: exist for every known type of particle; possess opposite properties, such as charge.

Pair production: creation of a particle and its corresponding antiparticle from a high-energy photon.

its particle counterpart, they annihilate each other to release two photons in opposite directions. A high-energy photon is capable of producing a particle–antiparticle pair in a process known as **pair production**. For every antiparticle swallowed up by a black hole, the particle counterpart would be emitted to form part of a stream of radiation away from the black hole. The mass of the black hole would be steadily reduced as a result of swallowing antiparticles at the same time as it emits a stream of radiation. The energy of this radiation is a measure of the temperature of the black hole.

The smaller the mass of the black hole, the higher its temperature is and the quicker it evaporates. Hawking worked out that the time taken to evaporate is longer than the age of the oldest stars if the mass is more than about 10^{12}kg. The Schwarzschild radius corresponding to this mass is about the same diameter as the nucleus of an atom. A black hole at the centre of a galaxy is much more massive and will be there for a long long time, dragging in surrounding matter which emits high energy radiation as it accelerates towards the event horizon.

EVIDENCE FOR BLACK HOLES

The two examples below could be explained by means other than black holes. However, black holes offer the most convincing explanations to date of the observations.

Cygnus X$_1$

This is an X-ray-emitting object of about six solar masses in a binary system. The object could be a black hole drawing matter from its companion. According to this theory, X-rays are emitted from matter as it is accelerated towards the event horizon. Other similar X-ray sources have been detected. The X-rays from these sources and from Cygnus X$_1$ fluctuate rapidly, indicating such sources are no larger than a few kilometres in diameter, perhaps caused by the collapse of a star more than twenty times as massive as the Sun.

M$_{87}$

This is a giant galaxy with an active nucleus that is very bright. Part of the galactic centre is spinning so fast that it is thought to contain an object of mass about three thousand million stars in a region no more than the size of the solar system.

✳ ✳ ✳ ✳SUMMARY ✳ ✳ ✳ ✳

The key rules for a black hole.

1 The Schwarzchild radius defines a sphere surrounding a black hole which no object or light can escape from.

2 The event horizon of a black hole is the surface of the Schwarzschild sphere surrounding a black hole. Events inside the event horizon cannot be seen outside the event horizon.

3 Thermal radiation from a black hole due to particle–antiparticle pairs created just outside the event horizon causes a black hole to evaporate. The rate of evaporation of a black hole is insignificant unless its mass is less than 10^{12} kg.

Einstein and the Big Bang

Few ideas have caught our imagination more than the idea that the Universe itself originated in a cataclysmic explosion, the Big Bang, and has continued to expand ever since. In this chapter, we look at the crucial part played by Einstein that led to the Big Bang Theory, and at the scientific evidence for this theory and why scientists estimate it happened about 12,000 million years ago. When he applied his General Theory of Relativity to cosmology, the science of the Universe, Einstein was following a long tradition that dates back to the earliest recorded attempts to explain the Universe, which we will examine here. We will also look at alternative theories and why these theories were discarded. Old theories in science sometimes reappear, albeit in a modified form – science can be much more mysterious than science fiction!

BEFORE THE BIG BANG THEORY

The Universe is thought to be expanding, causing every galaxy to move away from every other galaxy like dots on the surface of an expanding balloon. The astronomer Edwin Hubble discovered in 1929 that the further away a galaxy is, the faster it is receding from us. The Expanding Universe Theory explains Hubble's law and other observations. As we will see later in this chapter, the theory has also led scientists to deduce that the Universe originated about 10–12 billion years ago and to make predictions about the fate of the Universe. Newton, and other great scientists before Einstein, had no evidence that the Universe is expanding. Newton thought that the Universe was infinite, reckoning that if it was finite then the stars could not be stationary as otherwise they would all be attracted by each other's gravity into a great mass. The notion that they are rushing away from each other would prevent the collapse, of a finite universe but Newton had no evidence for such motion. An infinite universe would not suffer a collapse as any star would be attracted equally in all directions by all the other stars. The stars in an infinite Universe would need to be motionless though, because if the distance between a star and a neighbour less due to their movement, they will attract each other and collide, attracting other stars to them which would attract even more stars. An infinite Universe would be in a state of eternal collapse if the stars were not static. So Newton settled for a static and infinite Universe where the laws he discovered prevailed and where order reigned.

Newton's Universe went unchallenged for over a century until a very simple problem was raised which became known as Olber's Paradox. This is based on a very simple observation, namely that the night sky is dark not light! This seemingly trivial observation was first analysed by Heinrich Olbers in 1826. He proved mathematically that the sky would be permanently bright if the Universe consisted of an infinite number of stars. The fact that the sky is dark at night means that there is not an infinite number of stars in the Universe. Olbers originally thought that the Universe is infinite and unchanging. However, his analysis showed that this cannot be so. He reasoned that the Universe must be finite because the sky is dark. Since a finite static universe would collapse, Olbers reckoned it must be expanding.

EINSTEIN'S ERROR

If space is curved, a light ray could eventually return to the light source from which it was emitted, in the same way that a long-range aircraft on a journey round the world returns to its starting point. The surface of the Earth is an example of a curved two-dimensional surface that is finite and without any edge or boundary. Einstein used his General Theory of Relativity to predict that a finite, static Universe without boundaries is possible, like the Earth' surface except in four dimensions not two. To achieve this result, Einstein had to introduce a new type of repulsive force which acted only over a cosmological scale into his equations. This repulsive force was thought necessary by Einstein to overcome the force of attraction due to gravity that would make a finite static universe collapse.

Einstein introduced this force from his equations by means of a 'constant of integration' which became known as the cosmological constant, represented by the symbol λ. Unlike the inverse square law of gravity, Einstein worked out that the magnitude of the cosmological force increases with distance:

Cosmological force = $\frac{1}{3}\lambda r$ where r represents distance.

Einstein appreciated that λ could be positive, negative or zero. A negative value would hasten the collapse of a static Universe. Einstein worked out that a zero value would also lead to collapse. A positive value would prevent the collapse. So Einstein decided that the cosmological constant was necessary and it ought to be sufficiently positive to prevent the gravitational collapse of the Universe. Just as a balloon is prevented from collapsing by its internal pressure, so a cosmological repulsive force was thought necessary by Einstein to keep the Universe static.

Einstein's model of the Universe seemed to be self-consistent with no internal contradictions. The presence of the cosmological constant though made fellow theoreticians uneasy as it seemed to be an unjustified 'fiddle factor' which was not in keeping with the rigour and elegance of the General Theory of Relativity. Hubble's discovery that the distant galaxies are receding increased the unease. The problem of the cosmological constant emerged in 1927 when Georges Lemaitre, a Belgian priest and mathematician, discovered 'expanding Universe' solutions to Einstein's equations without the necessity of the cosmological constant. Lemaitre also discovered that his solutions had been worked out five years earlier by the Russian mathematician Alexander Friedmann who died in 1925 before his work became known. In recognition of Friedmann's contributions, the solutions are known as Freidmann models. His most interesting model is one in which the Universe expands then contracts.

Not surprisingly, the Church began to take an open-minded interest in the work of cosmologists again, several centuries after banning Galileo for teaching the Copernican model, and Lemaitre became President of the Pontifical Academy of Sciences. Although Einstein described the introduction of λ as 'the biggest blunder of my life', it has been resurrected in recent decades the Universe is older.

Constants of integration

Integration is the process of adding changes together to give the total change. A constant of integration is always part of the solution of any mathematical equation involving the rate of change of a quantity. For example, the rate of increase of velocity of an object due to gravity only just above the ground is –9.8 m/s^2, represented by the symbol g. The minus sign is necessary if we adopt the '+ is upwards, – is downwards' convention.

* This may be written as an equation in the form $\underline{dv} = g$, where g = –9.8m/s^2 and $\underline{d}$ means rate of change. $\overline{dt}$

* The increase of velocity, Δv, of an object in free fall is therefore gt, where t is the time in seconds from its release.

* Δv = gt. The actual velocity at time t after release is the initial velocity, u, plus the change of velocity Δv.

* v = u + gt where u is a constant of integration, equal to the intial velocity of the object. The initial velocity u can be positive (i.e. projected), negative (i.e. projected down) or zero (i.e. released at rest).

THE BEGINNING OF TIME

In 1929, the astronomer Edwin Hubble (1889–1953) published his discovery from observations of more than 20 galaxies that the speed of recession, υ, of a distant galaxy increases with its distance d from us, in according with the equation:

υ = Hd where H is the Hubble constant.

Many more observations have been made on more galaxies since then, leading to the conclusion that **Hubble's law** holds for galaxies as far away as 5,000 million light years. The value

KEYWORD

Hubble's law: states that the velocity of recession of a galaxy if in proportion to how far away it is.

of H is thought to be about 20 km/s per million light years. A galaxy at a distance of 5,000 million light years away would therefore be receding from us at a speed of 100,000 km/s (= 5000 x 20 km/s), about one third of the speed of light. On this basis, a galaxy receding at almost the speed of light would therefore be at a distance of no more than 15,000 million light years.

At the time of writing, work continues using the Hubble Space Telescope (HST) to measure the distances to supernovae billions of light years away. This will enable the Hubble constant to be determined accurately out to much greater distances than at present, instead of being extrapolated. The results thus far indicate a value of H of about 20 km/s per million light years although there is some evidence for a slight increase at the furthest distances of the order of 5,000 million light years. Perhaps this indicates an accelerated expansion of the Universe, although many more measurements need to be made to obtain firm evidence.

The Expanding Universe Theory, devised by Friedmann from the Einstein's Theory of General Relativity provides an explanation of Hubble's law. Based on a value of H of 20 km/s per million light years, the model leads to the conclusion that the Universe originated about 12,000 million years ago in a massive explosion, the Big Bang, throwing matter and radiation outwards from the point of its creation. What preceded the Big Bang, or what surrounded the point of creation, are questions beyond the present realms of science, as space time was created by the expansion of the Universe and so cannot be said to have existed before the Big Bang.

EVIDENCE FOR THE BIG BANG THEORY

If the number of stars is not infinite, gravitational attraction between galaxies would cause the Universe to collapse unless either it is expanding, as Olbers deduced (in which case gravity would reduce or eventually stop the rate of expansion), or else matter must be created continuously to prevent it collapsing. This latter theory, known as the Steady State Theory of the Universe was supported by many prominent scientists until recently, in spite of Hubble's law. In 1928, the famous astronomer Sir James Jeans spoke of 'points at the centres of nebulae where matter is continually poured into our Universe from some other dimension', and this view was still maintained by many eminent scientists until the 1960s. The Steady State Theory was developed from Jeans' ideas by Hermann Bondi, Thomas Gold and Fred Hoyle in 1948. The theory assumed that the Universe on a sufficiently large scale is the same at all locations and at all times. Assuming the Hubble constant does not change, the theory required the continuous creation of matter to make up for the spreading out of matter due to expansion. Points of creation referred to as white holes were envisaged, the opposite to black holes.

The reason for their support of the Steady State Theory lay in the discrepancy between the age of stars in globular clusters and the age of the Universe as estimated from the Hubble constant. At the time the Steady State Theory was put forward, the Hubble constant was thought to be such as to generate an age of little more than four billion years for the Universe, assuming the Big Bang Theory is correct. Improved measurements reduced the value to the Hubble constant, giving an age for the Universe of about seven billion years, younger than the age of the oldest stars, which is reckoned to be about 12–15 billion years. Clearly those who argued in favour of the Steady State Theory were distinctly unimpressed by a Universe younger than its own stars! However, their difficulties in convincing the Big Bang theorists deepened when the results and conclusions from an extensive survey of radio sources was published in 1955 by Martin Ryle at Cambridge. Using a high-resolution radio telescope, Ryle proved that the concentration of radio sources increased at large distances. This finding weakened the basic principle of uniformity in the Steady State Theory, the idea that the Universe should be the same on a large scale everywhere. Further surveys over the next decade supported Ryle's discovery. The concentration of radio sources at large distances seemed to indicate an excess of radio galaxies at some time in the distant past.

The dispute between the two theories was settled unambiguously in favour of the Big Bang by two major discoveries in the following decade. The Big Bang Theory is now supported by very strong evidence based on these discoveries.

Microwave background radiation

Microwave background radiation from all directions in space was first detected by Arno Penzias and Robert Wilson in America in 1965. They converted a satellite receiver system into a detector for radio astronomy by fitting a large reflector horn to the system. When they came to test the modified system, they noticed background radiation was present whichever direction the horn was directed in. This microwave background radiation was the same in all directions. Even though their receiver horn was able to distinguish radio sources as close as one sixtieth of a degree, they found the radiation was the same right round the sky. The discovery was taken up by other scientists and within a few months, the spectrum of the radiation had been measured and found to be the same as the thermal radiation spectrum of a body at a temperature of 2.9 degrees above absolute zero. the lowest possible temperature.

The presence of microwave background radiation is inexplicable in terms of the Steady State Theory of the Universe. There is no reason for its existence according to Steady State Theory. However, the Big Bang Theory does provide a natural explanation as the radiation is thought to be radiation released in the Big Bang that became longer and longer in wavelength as the Universe expanded. The energy, and hence the frequency, of the photons of radiation released in the Big Bang would have been very high, corresponding to a temperature of billions of degrees. According to the Big Bang Theory, as the Universe expanded, it became cooler and the radiation was stretched out more and more as the Universe expanded. The wavelength of the radiation therefore became longer and longer, and is now about 1mm at peak intensity.

Stars and galaxies

Stars and galaxies contain about three times as much hydrogen as helium. This observation can be explained as a consequence of the cooling of the Universe after the Big Bang. Above a temperature of 10,000 million degrees, neutrons and protons break free from nuclei. As the Universe cools, neutrons and protons joined to form helium nuclei at 10,000 million degrees, leaving excess protons as hydrogen nuclei. Because there were 14 protons for every 2 neutrons before the nuclei of atoms were formed, each helium nucleus locked up 2 protons and 2 neutrons, leaving 12 excess protons as hydrogen nuclei, corresponding to a hydrogen-to-helium mass ratio of three to one.

Why should there have been seven times as many protons as neutrons when the early Universe was at a temperature of 10,000 million degrees? The answer to this question lies in the fact that the neutron is slightly heavier than the proton and therefore the energy associated with its rest mass is slightly larger than for the proton. Protons and neutrons are made up of smaller particles called **quarks**. More energy is needed to form a neutron than a proton so the formation of a proton is more likely than the formation of a neutron. This energy difference is about the same as the kinetic energy of a proton or a neutron at a temperature of about 10,000 million degrees, and is just enough to account statistically for the fact that there is approximately one neutron for every seven protons.

KEYWORD

Quarks: fundamental partocles that make up protons and neutrons. As the universe expanded after the Big Bang, it cooled and quarks and antiquarks formed from high-energy radiation. More quarks and antiquarks were formed and the antiquarks were annihilated by the quarks. As the Universe cooled even more, the remaining quarks formed protons and neutrons.

Explanation of Hubble's Law

The Big Bang Theory of the origin of the Universe leads to the expanding model of the Universe which provides an explanation of Hubble's law. The Steady State Theory of the Universe requires the continuous creation of matter to explain Hubble's Law. There is no evidence for the continuous creation of matter. Also, the Steady State Theory cannot explain the microwave background or the hydrogen-to-helium ratio.

✻ ✻ ✻ ✻SUMMARY ✻ ✻ ✻ ✻

- Hubble's law states that the speed of recession of a distant galaxy is proportional to its distance.

- Models of the Universe.

1 Newton's Universe is static and infinite.

2 Einstein's static Universe requires the introduction a cosmological force of repulsion.

3 Friedmann's Universe expands without the necessity of a cosmological force.

4 The Steady State Theory supposes that matter is continuously created as matter spreads out.

5 The Big Bang Theory supposes that the Universe was created in an explosion at a point billions of years ago, and has been expanding ever since.

- Evidence in support of the Big Bang Theory.

1 Microwave background radiation from all directions in space is radiation from the Big Bang..

2 The ratio of hydrogen to helium: correct explanation of why there is three times as much hydrogen as helium in the Universe.

3 Explanation of Hubble's law.

An Uncertain End

After 1919, Einstein worked on the problem of how to bring quantum theory into the scope of general relativity. Philosophically, he parted company with most other scientists because he disapproved of the introduction of the idea of probability underpinning quantum theory. Until he settled in America in 1933, he responded positively to many invitations to lecture abroad and made a great impression on most people he met, regardless of their scientific background. He spoke out against the mood of anti-Semitism that was developing in Germany and he became a target of right-wing nationalists who attempted to discredit his scientific theories. His lack of success on a unified theory did not deter him from continuing to work on it, perhaps directed by his single-minded attitude. In this final chapter, we will look at aspects of Einstein's work that continue to preoccupy scientists today.

NATURAL UNCERTAINTY

The nature of light was shown by Einstein to be particle-like, as Newton had imagined two centuries before. An experiment on the passage of light from a narrow light source through two closely space slits had helped to prove that light has a wave like nature (see page 13). Einstein's photon theory of light, which was successfully tested by Millikan, led to the hypothesis that

light has a dual nature which is either wave-like or particle-like. This dual nature was predicted for matter particles by Louis de Broglie in France in 1923 and was confirmed within a few years when it was observed that electrons in a beam are diffracted by a thin crystal just as X-ray photons are. In an attempt to explain this dual behaviour, the idea of probability was introduced through the concept of a **probability amplitude**, like the amplitude of a wave, to find the most likely location of a particle. To explain a dark fringe in the double slits interference pattern described on page 13, each photon is said to have a probability amplitude due to the route via one slit and a probability amplitude due to the other route. A dark fringe is produced where the two probability amplitudes cancel each other out.

Einstein could not support the probability idea because he felt uneasy about natural processes being uncertain. This stance is summed up by his famous statement that 'God does not play dice'. In spite of the many advances and applications of quantum theory, he maintained this view throughout his life, seeking to the end a **deterministic theory** that would tie in quantum theory with relativity. As far as Einstein

KEYWORD

Deterministic theory: the philosophical idea that all events are fully determined by previous events. In quantum theory, an event is changed by the action of observing the event.

was concerned, uncertainty and probability are descriptions necessary only because the underpinning causes are not known. The notion that a particle or a photon might be in more than one place at the same time would seem to mean it has more than one possible path through space time which did not appeal to Einstein. The quantum theory still remains distinct from the General Theory of Relativity, almost fifty years after Einstein's death. High-energy particle experiments are likely to provide more clues about the nature of mass and energy and thereby provide a deeper understanding of the nature of space, time and the quantum world.

THE FATE OF THE UNIVERSE

Will the expansion of the Universe continue for ever or will it stop and reverse? By applying Einstein's general relativity equations to a model Universe consisting of uniformly-distributed dust, the expanding Universe was predicted by both Friedmann and Lemaitre. As we saw on page 74, Einstein introduced the cosmological constant into his model of the Universe to prevent its collapse due to gravity. Friedmann went on to discover an expanding Universe solution which did not need a cosmological constant.

Let us now look at what the expanding Universe solution tells us about the future of the Universe, starting with the idea of cosmic time which is that the Universe looks the same from any location at the same cosmic time. The importance of this simple idea is recognized by calling it cosmological principle.

The distance to any galaxy increases with time and will continue to do so. A model of how the distance to any galaxy changes with time must be based on consideration of the galaxies at the same cosmic time. A false picture would be obtained if one galaxy was considered at its position a billion years ago and another galaxy was considered at its position five billion years ago.

The changing distance between two galaxies may be expressed as an equation of the form: $d(t) = R(t)d_0$ where $d(t)$ is the distance at time t after the distance was d_0, and $R(t)$ is called the scale factor (see Appendix 3). This factor is not constant and changes with cosmic time. If $R(t)$ decreases in the future, the Universe will stop expanding and shrink. The Hubble constant H is equal to the rate of increase of the scale factor divided by the scale factor. Thus H is a parameter that changes with time and isn't a universal constant. How the Hubble constant changes with time therefore depends on how the scale factor changes with time. More measurements of H from galaxies further and further away will provide clues as to how the scale factor and thus the Universe might develop.

What does Einstein's General Theory of Relativity tell us about how the scale factor changes with time? The outcome, according to the Friedmann–Lemaitre model, supports the theory that the Universe is expanding but it predicts three possible futures, depending on the overall density of matter in the Universe. If the density of matter in the Universe is greater than a certain value known as the critical density, the Universe faces a hot future and an eventual end in the so-called Big Crunch. The critical density is the least density that would allow the Universe to expand to infinity. If the density of the Universe is smaller than the critical density, the Universe will expand forever, the so-called Big Yawn scenario.

Figure 14: The Big Crunch

* If the density of matter in the Universe is greater than the critical density, the Universe will collapse, corresponding to a closed Universe. In this case, the curvature of space is positive, like that of a surface (e.g. a sphere) that curves back round on itself.

* If the density of matter in the Universe is equal to the critical density, the Universe will continue to expand, eventually stopping at infinity. This scenario corresponds to a flat Universe, like a surface of zero curvature (i.e. a plane) that stretches to infinity.

* If the density of matter in the Universe is less than the critical density, the Universe will continue to expand without stopping , corresponding to an open Universe. The curvature of space in this case is negative, unable to stop the expansion of the Universe.

THE BIG CRUNCH?
The critical density of the Universe corresponds to about half-a-dozen protons per cubic metre. Hydrogen and helium make up most of the luminous matter of the Universe. The density of such matter is reckoned to be about 0.01 x the critical density. This estimate is based on the measurement of the intensity of the cosmic background microwave

radiation. This yields an estimate of 400 million photons per cubic metre of space. The theory of nucleosynthesis explains satisfactorily the observation that the Universe contains 25% helium to 75% hydrogen. This theory also predicts that one proton or neutron is produced for every 10,000 million photons. From these two facts, we can deduce that the Universe contains about 0.04 proton or neutrons per cubic metre, well below several protons per cubic metre required for the critical density.

Galaxies are known to contain **dark matter** which is matter that does not emit detectable electromagnetic radiation. The mass-to-light ratio of a galaxy is 10–100 times the mass-to-light ratio of the Sun, indicating the presence of dark matter 10–100 times more abundant than luminous matter in galaxies. In addition, **galactic rotation** studies indicate the presence of hidden mass in the halo that is thought to envelop the galactic disc. Another indicator of the presence of dark matter are the distorted images caused by light from a distant galaxy being bent by an intervening cluster of galaxies. The size of the image is a measure of the mass of the cluster causing the deflection. The results of such investigations indicate far more

KEYWORDS

Dark matter: hidden matter in space that cannot be detected except by its gravitational effect. Rotating galaxies are slowed down by the presence of dark matter.

Galactic rotation: galaxies, such as the Milky Way and Andromeda, are known to be rotating. However, the measured rate of rotation is much less than the rate of rotation calculated according to the mass of the stars of the galaxy.

mass in such clusters than its luminosity suggests. Overall, the Universe is thought to contain about ten times as much dark matter as ordinary (i.e. luminous) matter. In other words, approximately 90% of the mass of the Universe is in the form of dark matter. If this is the case, the overall density of matter in the Universe is ten times greater than the density of ordinary matter, corresponding to about 0.4 protons per cubic metre which is still well below the critical density. On the basis of evidence thus far, the Universe would therefore seem to be open, expanding forever heading for the Big Yawn! However, astronomers are searching for hidden mass in other forms. The Sun and all the stars produce billions of billions of highly elusive particles called neutrinos every second as a result of fusing hydrogen into helium. The rest mass of the neutrino is too small to measure at present. If it is found to be more than about 50 billionths (i.e. 0.05 millionths) of the rest mass of a proton, the Universe is in for a sticky end in a Big Crunch!

EINSTEIN CONCLUDED

Einstein would have found the work of today's scientists fascinating. As a scientist, he moved onto the sidelines in his pursuit of a unified theory but he remained a public figure, particularly after the use of the atom bomb in 1945 when he wrote to President Roosevelt urging an international ban on such weapons. After his formal retirement, he continued to work on cosmology with his successors at Princeton and on the unified theory problem. He had become a US citizen in 1940, four years after the death of his second wife Elsa, a marriage that had lasted 17 years. In 1952, he turned down an informal offer of the Presidency of the State of Israel, perhaps aware that the prestige his international status might bring to the post would be more than offset by his lack of political experience, although more likely intent on pursuing his scientific interests which he maintained until a few days before he died on 18 April 1955.

Looking back over Einstein's life, it seems clear that his theories of special and general relativity mark him out as the greatest scientist since Newton. His single-minded pursuit of a deeper understanding of nature might seem at odds with the image of an absent-minded professor which he sometimes liked to present to the world. His relativity theories were the product of intense thought coupled with enormous insight and intuition in physics which guided his mathematical work and which left science with a totally different conceptual framework to the absolute world of Newton. Future generations will undoubtedly remember Einstein, long after the tumultuous events of the twentieth century become part of a distant age.

Appendix 1 More about Special Relativity

Consider the progress of a light wave spreading out from a point source. If an observer who is stationary relative to the light source could see the wave spreading out, passing distance markers as it progressed, he or she would observe its distance from the point source increasing with time, according to the equation:

Distance moved r = speed of light c x time t

To keep the analysis simple, imagine the distance markers are in two perpendicular directions only: east and north. We will use x for one of these distances (east) and y for the other (north). Using Pythagoras, theorem, $r^2 = x^2 + y^2$, we can see that $x^2 + y^2 = c^2 t^2$ (we will call this equation 1)

A second observer moving at speed, υ relative to the first observer in the x-direction would make measurements using his or her own coordinate system to arrive at a similar equation:

distance moved r' = speed of light c x time t'

where r' and t' are measurements made by the second observer.

Using x' and y' for this observer's two coordinate system therefore gives us equation 2: $x'^2 + y'^2 = c^2 t'^2$.

If the two observers started off at the same point, according to Newton's ideas of space and time, then:

* $x' = x - \upsilon t$
* $y' = y$
* $t' = t$

Substituting the expressions for x', y' and t' into equation 2 will not give equation 1. Using Newton's ideas, it's not possible to transform one equation into the other. What Einstein did was to derive the set of transformation formulae below to transform one equation into the other:

* $x' = \gamma (x - \upsilon t)$

* $y' = y$ (the y-coordinate isn't affected by motion in the x-direction)

* $t' = \gamma \left(t - \dfrac{\upsilon x}{c^2}\right)$ where $\gamma = \dfrac{1}{\sqrt{\left(1 - \dfrac{\upsilon^2}{c^2}\right)}}$

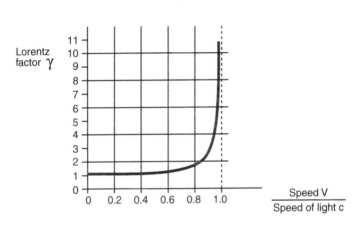

Figure 15: The Lorentz factor

The Lorentz factor is the key to why nothing can travel faster than light. Figure 15 shows how γ changes with speed υ. It increases from 1 at zero speed and it becomes infinitely large at $\upsilon = c$.

Appendix 2 The Einstein Tensor

The Einstein tensor represents the difference between the curvature in a certain direction along a certain line at a given point, R_{ij}, and the local curvature, R, at that point taking the 'weighting factor' for directions into account. In precise terms, $E_{ij} = R_{ij} - \frac{1}{2} g_{ij} R$. The local curvature R is an invariant as it does not depend on the coordinate system used.

On the golf course

Imagine a hill where there is a small patch marked out by four posts. The edges of the patch are defined by the shortest lines between adjacent posts. Any point P in the patch could be located by two coordinates measured from one of the posts, one coordinate x_1 being the distance to the nearest point along one edge from P, and the other coordinate x_2 being the corresponding distance along the other edge from P. The gradient at a point on the hill depends on direction. Remember that the curvature along any line is determined by the change of gradient at two nearby points along the line.

* The curvature tensor R_{ij} is the curvature at a point determined from the change of the gradient in the direction of coordinate axis x_i, between two points along coordinate axis x_j, where $_i$ and $_j$ = 1 or 2 or 3 or 4.

* The local curvature R is worked out using a weighted contribution from each component of the curvature tensor R_{ij}.

* $^1\!/_2\, g_{ij}$ R is half the value of the local curvature after weighting it with g_{ij} to take account of how much $\delta x_i\, \delta x_j$ contributes to δs^2.

* So E_{ij} represents how much more or less the curvature in a certain direction along a certain line is in comparison with the local curvature at that point.

Appendix 3 The Scale Factor R(t)

The distance between two galaxies at cosmic time t, $d(t) = R(t)\, d_0$, where d_0 is the present distance.

The speed of recession $v(t)$ is the rate of change of distance which is therefore the rate of change of the scale factor, to be written $R'(t)$, multiplied by d_0:

$v(t) = R'(t) d_0$

Combining the two equations to eliminate d_0 gives $v(t) = \dfrac{R'(t)}{R(t)}\, d(t)$

This may be written in the form of Hubbe's law:

$v(t) = H\, d(t)$

with $\dfrac{R'(t)}{R(t)}$ equal to the Hubble constant H.

This analysis shows that H is a parameter that changes with time. How the Hubble constant changes with time depends on how the scale factor changes.

INDEX